Wapitis
Wellingtons
and Binderband

From farming to flying via crash landings & carpentry,
Wings made his mark on our world

Written by
Roger Maw and his family

First Published in Great Britain in 2014 by Tucann Books
Text © Joss Blakey All rights reserved
Design © TUCANN*design&print*

The authors Joss, Mike and Tessa wish to point out that all the fond memories
relating to the compilation of this book are as acurate as humanly possible.

ISBN **978-1-907516-29-0**

Produced by: TUCANN*Limited*,
19 High Street, Heighington Lincoln LN4 1RG
Tel & Fax: 01522 790009
www.tucann.co.uk

ACKNOWLEDGEMENTS
—————AND THANKS—————

To my brother, Mike, for collecting so much information on father's life.

My sister, Tess, for her memories and encouragement.

My sister in law Patricia for the title.

My cousin Jill for her illustration of the goons in the prison camp.

My niece, Sam, for her computer work.

Roger's friends and family with their vivid memories that brought this book to life.

My cousins Jill, Ursula, Nicola and Jo for their vivid memories of Cleatham, their Uncle Roger and riding in his 'aeroplane car'.

The instructors, riggers and fitters who kept him flying safely most of the time!

Albert Simpson whose memories of India and flying with Roger are priceless.

David Lee who flew in India at the same time as Roger. His vivid memories brought Roger's Indian photo album to life. David Lee wrote 'Never Stop the Engine when it's Hot'.

Information from the Oundle School archivist.

Wapitis, Wellingtons and Binderband

Lauren, the star of archives in RAF Hendon Museum, who supplied the programme of the RAF Air Display, 27 June 1931.

Anne Scott for finding pictures of ancient places online.

The Garvey family for their friendship and memories.

Squadron Leader Young, MBE for his great memories of 503 Squadron.

Artie Hawbrook for his POW newspapers and memorabilia of The Dambusters and D Day.

Joan Woolhouse for rescuing Roger from the ditch and giving our parents such a good quality of life in their later years.

Tom Cann at Tucann who looked at my brother's collection and said 'Someone needs to write the story', and then printed the book for us.

Ernest G Hardy for all his research on the operations record books of 142, 12 and 108 Squadrons during Roger's time with them.

Audrey Grealy for her poem 'Stalag Luft'.

Olly Philpot for his friendship and super book 'Stolen Journey'.

Eric Williams for his book 'The Wooden Horse'.

Les Sidwell for his book 'Wingless Journey'.

Peter Green for his splendid photographic collection and the book 'Wings over Lincolnshire' which he wrote with Mike Hodgson and Bill Taylor.

RAF Waddington for archive photographs and their book 'For Faith and Freedom'.

Martin Bowman who wrote 'Wellington: The Geodetic Giant' with its fascinating photographs.

F R Chappell who wrote 'Wellington Wings' bringing The Muddle East to life.

Wing Commander Ken Rees, a Great Escaper, whose book 'Lie in the Dark and Listen' supplied a photograph of The Great Escapers' memorial.

Pictures of a room and POWs cooking in Stalag Luft 3 from 'The Last Escape' by John Nichol and Tony Rennell.

Information from 'Stalag Luft III: The Secret Story' by Arthur Durand.

James next door who showed me how to make a paragraph on the computer when I first started my bit of this book, and - to the West Suffolk College, Mildenhall branch who taught me slowly over many weeks how to use a computer as a word processor.

Most of all to Judy Robertson who deserves a Bletchley medal for interpreting my scrawl and printing it accurately when I was writing faster than my computer skills could cope with.

CONTENTS

Cleatham

—CLEATHAM DAYS—

Roger Hargreaves Maw was born on June 24th 1906 into the secure hard-working world of a Lincolnshire farm. The first people he knew were his mother Lucy, his father Arthur and Emma who helped his mother to run the busy household, look after his eldest brother John, twelve year old sister Dulcie and his brother Dick.

He was christened in Manton Church where the ancestors' graves lay in rows outside the west wall. As soon as Roger was able to move around his cot it was clear he was to become a determined character - Lucy had to send down to the farmyard for a clean pig net to prevent him from climbing out.

Roger safe in mother's arms

John, Dick, Dulcie and Roger with Mother

Roger with Emma

As Roger's small world enlarged he grew to love his parents, Emma and his explorations into the garden and farmyard where he met Skipworth the gardener who had 17 children, and Law the garthman who milked the cows and had 16 children. They lived in small cottages on the farm as did the shepherds and carters who worked and cared for the 25 Shire horses. Arthur bred some of the finest prize winning Shires.

The garden was a grand place for a boy to play in, with shrubberies for stalking tigers and making dens and a huge swing near the gate whose iron ropes went up for ever into an old beech tree - it was a bit like flying. Lucy loved her garden and the children knew they had to respect the rose beds and to be careful not to damage the conservatory with its big old grape vine and smell of damp ferns.

Cleatham garden, the edge of the boys' world

One of Roger's favourite occupations was to follow Marshall the carpenter about as he repaired windows, doors, carts and even making a chaise longue frame for Lucy to upholster and button. Young Roger watched the intricacies of dovetailing joints and repairing the ropes in sash window frames, soon learning that nothing was impossible for Marshall. When Roger was too busy in his farm world to return to the house there was always the five seater privy in the farmyard - one of the seats was just his height.

As he grew older his toys included clockwork trains with tracks to put together. Roger and his brothers would take the controlling governor off the train to make it go faster.

Lucy and gardener Skipworth in the rose garden

Many winter hours in the playroom were happily absorbed by his Meccano set, but his pride and joy was a real steam engine.

Roger loved being out of doors and his mother's picnics were memorable. The pony and trap were brought round, Emma loaded a picnic basket in and they would set off for adventures. The bluebell woods were probably the first picnic of the year and the blackberrying ones included Lucy's walking stick to pull down the higher brambles, all the children, Emma and the little maids had many containers to fill. Harvest picnics would include gallons of Lucy's home brewed beer which she made for the harvesters with the help of one of the farmworkers wives. Several years later picnics were taken further afield in the big car and eaten sitting on the running board.

When young Roger mastered the art of riding a bicycle his world expanded greatly. He had a special container fitted to his cycle frame for yeast. Emma would say "Mester Roger will you go to the bakers in Kirton and get me some yeast this morning please." With the money safe in his trouser pocket he would cycle the 4 miles into Kirton Lindsey, pausing to watch the great steam trains puff into the station with fish fresh

10

from Grimsby, and visitors from far flung places, then up the steep hill to the bakers. Another favourite ride was to the Kirton windmill to see the great sails turning to work the huge gears for grinding the corn into flour for Emma's bread.

Visits by relations were always welcomed. Uncle Harold, Lucy's brother, farmed on the Isle of Axholme, but he was also in the Yeomanry, which Roger thought was a sort of auxiliary army. He would go to camp and help to train the new recruits. He once had the honour to welcome King Edward VII at a railway station. Overcome by the occasion he forgot his prepared speech and simply said "Oh King live forever," which seemed to please His Majesty. Lucy's sister Francie became Mrs Johnson when she married a chicken farmer, and their boy Ian was about Roger's age so the two boys were good friends and got into no end of scrapes together.

Roger on left with his cousin Ian

There were a lot of Stephenson relations of Lucy's. One visit that Roger, his sister and brothers had to behave especially well was to Great Aunts Kate and Maida. They were a little eccentric and during times of war they kept their silver and valuables in a Gladstone bag by the front door so they could pick it up and run from the enemy.

Uncle Harold Stephenson

Christmas dinner was the highlight of the Cleatham year. The great table laid with well-polished silver and glass and groaning with delicious home grown food that Emma and Lucy had worked tirelessly for weeks to prepare. The three Maw uncles came over from Walk House Farm. There was Uncle William who ran the farm and his wife Aunt Georgiana and Uncle Matthew an engineer with tales of India and the railways he had helped to construct there. Roger was fascinated by the huge stable clock he built. Every time it chimed the flag pole lit up as he had also installed electricity at Walk House by means of a windmill which charged a lot of accumulators in a shed near the house. Uncle George was a doctor married to Aunt Beatrice, they had three children Oliver, Vera and little Christine. The great Christmas dinner would seem to go on endlessly for small children wanting to play with their new toys, and they could not rely on Emma to take them off to play as she would need a well-earned rest before tackling the washing up.

Emma came to the Maw family with Lucy when she married. She started work at the age of 12 as a kitchen maid in Lucy's family home, and Grandpa Stephenson 'gave' her to Lucy along with new pots and pans for her new kitchen. Emma was delighted - she now rated a cap with streamers, and was given a lilac print dress for the wedding.

The First World War changed everyone's lives, Rogers's eldest brother John joined the Honourable Artillery Company and went off to Egypt. He sent home postcards with pictures of himself with his fellow officers and their horses.

Brother John in his new uniform

Uncle Harold went to train troops so Arthur made a weekly visit to his farm by bicycle. He would cycle to the River Trent, shout BO-AT as loud as he could, so the ferryman could row across to take him to the Isle of Axholme where he would cycle to the farm, discuss the farm work for the following week with the foreman, pay the men, and cycle back to the ferry where the ferryman would probably be working in his garden.

Several of the local factories began war work which included making planes.

Ruston Procter and Company built Sopwith Camel fuselages. This one is being hauled through the streets of Lincoln by Munitionettes - women doing war work in the Ruston factories for a recruitment drive.

The most exciting change was on the hilltop above Cleatham where a field became an airfield to guard the great steelworks of Scunthorpe against zeppelin raids. There was a hut, some planes and several young airmen. There was not much action against the enemy so they welcomed visits from the curly haired young cyclist, letting him sit in the cockpit and occasionally firing the gun.

Every Sunday the Maw boys put on their Sunday suits and the whole family drove in the horse and trap to Manton church. The sermons were long and boring for a small boy so Roger would make various shapes out of his white hanky - clean and ironed by Emma - until one awful day when the Vicar roared out "Roger Maw stop making rabbits out of your handkerchief." The shame, the disgrace, the trouble from parents. The

The pilots of B Flight, 33 (home Defence) Squadron in the Flight's operations room at Manton (Kirton in Lindsey) in late 1917. The Squadron had arrived in Lincolnshire at the end of 1916 for anti-Zeppelin duties and had established A, B and C Flights at Scampton, Manton and Elsham respectively. The three flights concentrated to Manton in June 1918 and with the diminished threat of Zeppelin attack, finished the war as a night training unit.
WJ Taylor collection

Avro 504 Night Fighters of 33 Squadron at Manton (Kiron in Lindsey) at the end of the war. The Avro 504s replaced the earlier FE.2 and Bristol Fighter aircraft in August 1918 and were only ever used for training purposes. Note the Holt flares just visible under the lower wing tips.
PHT Green collection

next Sunday Roger's Sunday suit was missing, and an extensive search by Emma, the two little maids and his mother proved fruitless, so he was sent happily to bed until their return from church. During the week it was found under the mat in the hall - quite flat.

The next Sunday the suit had mysteriously disappeared again - mats were raised everywhere but no sign of it. Once more he went happily to bed. The next week someone noticed a picture slightly askew, they straightened it and out fell the missing suit.

The next Sunday young Roger himself was missing - they called and searched high and low, and once more they went to church without him. He was eventually discovered in the big conservatory hiding under a bench fast asleep. Lucy said she could not put up with it. There was only one solution - they must go to Kirton Lindsey to the church there, it meant leaving a lot earlier and having lunch late but it could not be helped if it restored some peace of mind on a Sunday. From then on church was much more enjoyable. The Reverend Garvey once said in his sermon "We must not be just good people we must be *nice* people." The Garvey family of Trixie, Patsy, Vi and Ronald were also friends with another clergy family the Thorntons with Maurice and Janett from Corringham nearby. The young people became lifelong friends, visiting and playing together as they grew up.

All too soon it was time for Roger to go to school.

Roger in his new school coat

Until now formal schooling had been by various governesses who came and swiftly left as the boys teased them so much. The school in Derbyshire was full of large bullies who would roll the younger boys down the hill among the brambles for sport. Roger was very unhappy and sent home with pneumonia.

The next great journey with school trunk and tuck box crammed full by Emma was to Westerleigh Preparatory School at St Leonards-on-Sea on the south coast.

Westerleigh Cadets

16

The Headmaster inspired the boys by making a bridge - army style with rope and string and bits of wood - it all went well until the guy ropes were loosened and someone fell in the pond. War work for the boys consisted of knitting scarves for the soldiers, I doubt if Roger's ever got to the Front as he was constantly going back to Matron to retrieve dropped stitches.

The War ended, his brother John survived and came home amid much jubilation. He left the army and became a chartered accountant in London. The local factories ceased war work, several air fields were returned to the plough including Manton and Scampton. The many surplus planes were used for joy riding and exhibitions such as flying circuses.

Arthur did not send his two youngest sons to Rugby as he said the only thing he learned there was to ride a Penny Farthing bicycle, so Dick and Roger went to Oundle to join Laundimer House. Roger arriving at the school with another of Emma's specially packed tuck boxes in September 1920.

His first appearance on stage was as a goblin in The Tempest which was not an enjoyable experience, but he was interested in the stage lighting which came in for special mention in the school magazine. The Laxtonian, an excerpt from The Junior Play. December 14 and 15 1920 the Junior school in their usual triplicate manner produced Shakespeare's Tempest. Considerable energy on the part of the coaches, both verbal and instrumental at length reduced the early chaos to some sort of order, so the show given before the school was distinctly a success. The dance of the nymphs and reapers was accorded a triple encore, which was so vigorously given that at the end of the scene there was a considerable dispute among the apparently light and airy, but really most solid and earthly nymphs as to whose sandals were whose, but the stage had no splinters so it did not matter. Brooks as Stephano maintained a high level of vulgarity. Munton made quite a good Miranda when he ceased to hitch up his skirts as if they were trousers.

The lighting in the play was especially difficult, and our sincere thanks are due to Spilsbury and his satellites for the beautiful effects they produced. The alchemical effects in Prospero's cave with its fearsome feline inhabitant added considerably to the effect of the scene. Last but by no means least come Mr King and his myrmidons whose task was far from a light one, when overwhelmed by crowds of nymphs, goblins, and other such vermin; but they emerged unscathed.

Roger did not like singing, following his Uncle who declared he only knew two tunes, one was God Save the King and the other one was not. He did not like French either, do not say eh, say eh were the repetitive and incomprehensible instructions. Maths however was acceptable and he gained two prizes during his time at Oundle, and a lifelong understanding of ratios and how to work out stresses and strains which were to stand him in good stead.

Roger was confirmed by the Bishop of Peterborough in 1922 in the school chapel, his Christian foundations having been firmly laid by his parents, Emma, and the Reverend Garvey from Kirton Lindsey. He did not hide his suit on this occasion!

A great deal of fun was had in the school holidays with the Garveys and the Thorntons and friends. There were tennis parties in the summer, the front lawn at Cleatham was ideal as the spectators could sit in the shade of the tall trees on hot days, and Emma would provide gallons of homemade lemonade and a delicious tea. They went to dances together, and the young people took up amateur dramatics, which they performed in village halls as far away as Market Rasen - Roger becoming expert with scenery and lighting effects, Maurice Thornton being the leading actor. After one performance a lady came up to them and said the lighting in the last scene was so realistic, Roger thanked her and commented to his friends that she had not realised the scenery was on fire.

Roger's last year at Oundle was spent in the Farming class, and the demonstration for the parents at the end of the year included shoeing a horse. He was also a member of the Officers Training Corps. The inspecting Officer recorded "the contingent is well organised and trained with excellent discipline, and understanding of the rifle and Lewis gun." Out of 65 cadets who took the written exam Roger and 50 others passed their March A Certificate, a qualification that would be very useful in gaining entry to the Air Force later on.

Kirton Lindsey amateur dramatic club.

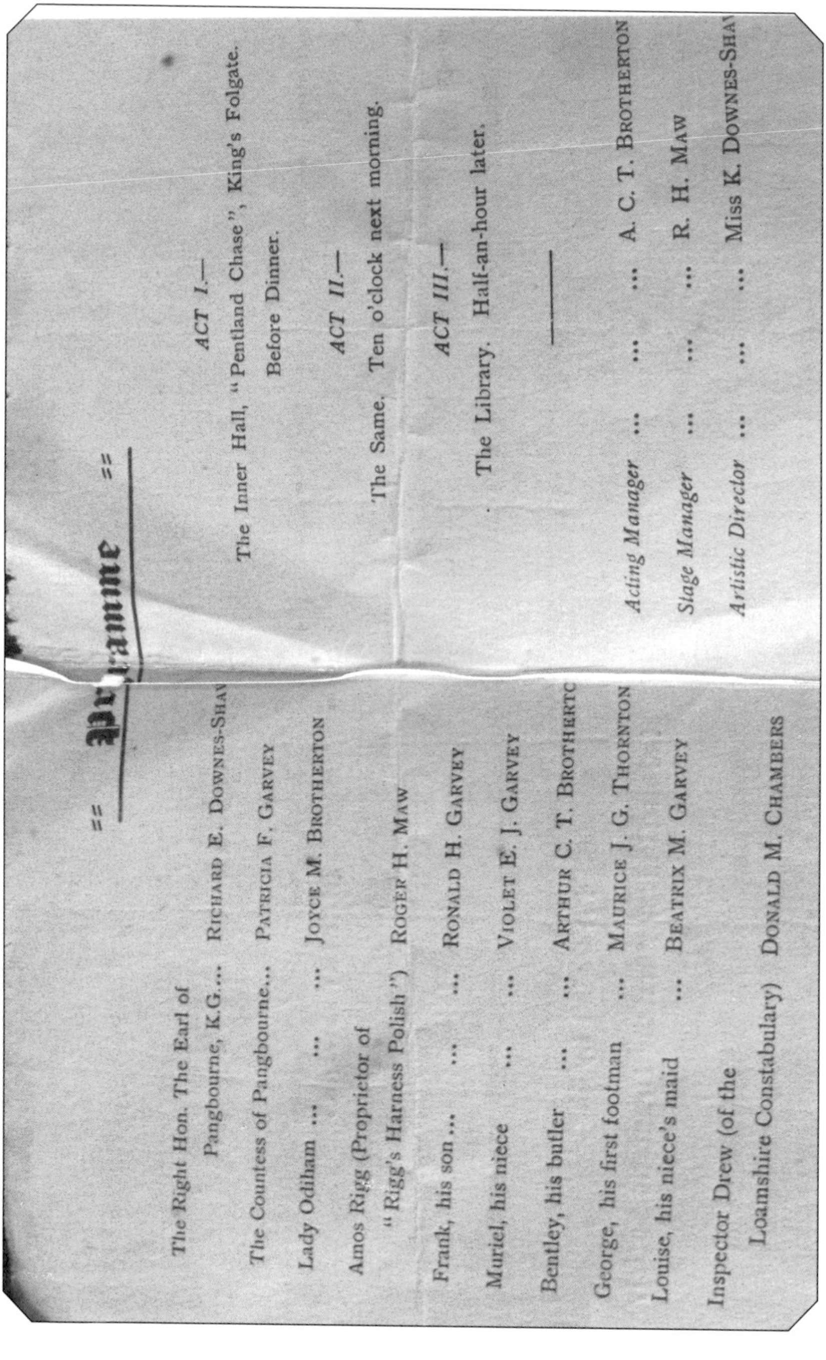

== Programme ==

The Right Hon. The Earl of
   Pangbourne, K.G.... RICHARD E. DOWNES-SHAW

The Countess of Pangbourne... PATRICIA F. GARVEY

Lady Odiham ... ... JOYCE M. BROTHERTON

Amos Rigg (Proprietor of
   "Rigg's Harness Polish") ROGER H. MAW

Frank, his son ... ... RONALD H. GARVEY

Muriel, his niece ... ... VIOLET E. J. GARVEY

Bentley, his butler ... ... ARTHUR C. T. BROTHERTON

George, his first footman ... MAURICE J. G. THORNTON

Louise, his niece's maid ... BEATRIX M. GARVEY

Inspector Drew (of the
   Loamshire Constabulary) DONALD M. CHAMBERS

ACT I.—

The Inner Hall, "Pentland Chase", King's Folgate.
Before Dinner.

ACT II.—

The Same. Ten o'clock next morning.

ACT III.—

The Library. Half-an-hour later.

Acting Manager ... ... A. C. T. BROTHERTON

Stage Manager ... ... R. H. MAW

Artistic Director ... ... Miss K. DOWNES-SHAW

School army cadet inspection at camp

When Roger left school and joined his father full time on the farm he persuaded him to buy a tractor, which was a great event in the area, as everyone worked the land with horses. The only machines on the farm so far had been the huge steam engines drawing the plough from one side of the field to the engine on the other side. Roger rode across on it one day, it was strange to hear just the earth turning over when he was away from the noise of the engines, but he could see the potential of untiring machines. Threshing time brought a steam engine to the farmyard again with its noise and power, whirling belts driving pulleys to rotate the threshing drum, golden grain pouring into sacks, and the straw walkers spewing the straw out of the back. It needed a large workforce to keep it going, fascinating for a boy to watch but hard work for so many men.

Roger soon mastered driving and maintaining the tractor. People came from miles around to see it. He spent many long hours ploughing and watching the white clouds of gulls that followed. One gull in particular he noticed as it only had one leg, he studied how it angled its wings in a different way according to the wind for a perfect landing each time.

Inspired by the success of the tractor, Arthur bought a car from a local maker, Ruston Hornsby in Lincoln, the number plate FL 221. It was a touring car, very big and heavy with a foldaway hood and large running boards which proved ideal for picnics.

Arthur, Lucy and Roger enjoying one of Emma's picnics with the Ruston Hornsby car

The brakes, however, were not too sharp, so Roger added an extension to the handle of the handbrake. When Arthur approached the stalls on Brigg market he would stand up while driving and haul on the handbrake. It was a technique he more or less mastered until a policeman walked in front of the car and was knocked down. Seeing the man scrambling to his feet, Arthur went to the nearest stall, removed a large turbot from the centre of the fishmonger's display and put it directly into the policeman's arms - "Mester Maw," he said, "you can knock me down any day of the week." The fishmonger was paid and no more was heard of the incident. Gradually cars were to be seen among the horses and bicycles, one or two motorbikes too.

Roger riding pillion on his motorbike

Roger and Maurice Thornton both had motorbikes and his sister Janett fearlessly rode pillion on her brother's motor bike scandalizing the little village, preparing them for the shock when she took over his old Clyno. One of the motorbikes was dressed up as a mouse for the Kirton Fete.

Maurice Thornton and Roger with the 'mouse' motorbike at the Kirton Fete

One day there was a most unusual visitor at Cleatham, he arrived unannounced on business. The little maid answered the door, "Who shall I say sir?" she asked. "Wing Commander Twistleton Wykeham Fiennes," was the reply. As this was quite beyond her she found Lucy and told her there was a gentleman to see her. The splendidly uniformed officer settled comfortably in the Drawing room and revealed his plans. "I am looking for young gentlemen to join the Auxiliary and Special Reserve Air Force and learn to fly. I understand your youngest son has left school." After some thought and many questions Arthur and Lucy gave their consent, and the gardener's boy was despatched to fetch Mister Roger from his beloved tractor. It was arranged after a firm but somewhat oily hand shake that he would report for instruction at weekends to Waddington aerodrome just beyond Lincoln. Transport was no problem as he had his trusty motorbike.

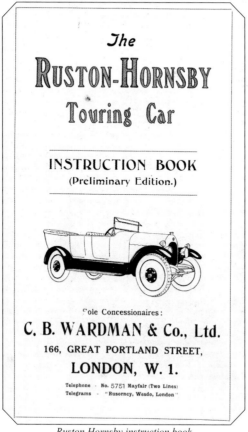

Ruston Hornsby instruction book

Roger relaxing, school days over, considering his future

OVER THE EDGE

May 1st 1927 Emma prepared a special breakfast of porridge and cream, bacon and eggs from the farm, toast and her best butter with marmalade. Roger and his father sat down to a real feast in the high ceilinged sunny kitchen discussing as they did every day the work on the farm, today however was different, Emma was carefully wrapping special goodies to go in Roger's bundle of clothes. He strapped it on the back of his motorbike, thanked Emma, hugged his Mother, kicked the bike into life and roared off towards Lincoln. The farmyard seemed strangely quiet as Arthur walked past the silent tractor to give the farm men their orders for the day.

Roger rode through Lincoln towards RAF Waddington which is situated like so many Lincolnshire airfields on the Lincoln Edge, a limestone escarpment overlooking the Trent valley, good for views and upcurrents. When he arrived there he found a well established grass aerodrome with some Royal Flying Corps hangars from the last war. As he parked his motorbike the three other trainee pilots came out of the Officers Mess to greet him.

They joined the regular officers and flying instructors, and were soon discussing planes and listening to tales of the Royal Flying Corps days. Such characters - there was Bachy Achelor who regularly flew through the hangar until someone shut the doors - he survived better than the plane but had a twisted neck. He swore he would continue flying until he twisted it straight again. Then there was the tale of ancient rivalry between a night flying squadron at Scampton and the Waddington one. One moonlit night a Scampton plane flew in quietly, the pilot and observer hastily planted a young fir tree in the middle of the grass in front of the

The first four Special Reservist Officers of 503 Squadron, May 1927. L-r T H Worth, D G Allison, N D Wardrop, R H Maw. Doug's first time in uniform. The tailplane J8516 is an Avro 504 that they would fly many times.

hangar before flying off swiftly undetected. Flying Instructor Wimpenny was teaching his pupils low flying, as one came in to land he rushed out to the plane, "Call that low flying," he shouted. "I'll show you low flying," and climbed into the cockpit, roared off over the fields nearby, returning with several sheaves of corn and the top of a five bar gate stuck in the undercarriage.

There were also instructors for training the reservist airmen as riggers and mechanics, a good combination with trainee pilots.

The aerodrome was equipped with Avro 504K *ab initio* trainers, and the Fairey Fawns, two seater day bomber biplanes which were first designed in 1921. A V Roe's works were nearby at Bracebridge Heath which was handy for spares and repairs.

There was a lot to learn. They were each issued a pilot's log book with printed instructions as to the correct terms to use when filling them in each time they flew. Several tests were mentioned for cross country flying, height and forced landing.

The Officers' Mess, Waddington, 1927

Rigging a biplane

Time carried forward :—

Date and Hour	Aeroplane Type and No.	Pilot	Passenger(s)	Time	H

CORRECT DESCRIPTION OF FLYING PRACTICES
FOR ENTRY IN REMARKS COLUMN OF PILOTS FLYING LOG BOOKS

PASSENGER FLYING,
TAXYING AND HANDLING ENGINE.
EFFECT OF CONTROLS WITH / WITHOUT ENGINE.
STRAIGHT FLYING LEVEL FLYING.
CLIMBING GLIDING, STALLING.
TAKING OFF INTO WIND
LANDING AND JUDGING DISTANCES.
TURNS UP TO 45 DEGREES.
AILERON DRAG
GLIDING TURNS
TURNS OVER 45 DEGREES WITH/WITHOUT ENGINE
SPINNING
ELEMENTARY FORCED LANDINGS
SOLO
CLIMBING TURNS
SIDE SLIPPING
TAKING OF AND LANDING ACROSS WIND
LOOPING
HALF ROLL
STALLING TURNS WITH / WITHOUT ENGINE.
FALLING LEAF
ADVANCED FORCED LANDINGS
LOW FLYING
FRONT SEAT FLYING
AIR PILOTAGE
PETROL SUPPLY. SWITCHING TANK TO TANK
FORCED LANDINGS, FAILURE OF STARBOARD OR PORT
   ENGINE (TWIN ENGINED AIRCRAFT ONLY)
CROSS COUNTRY TEST
PASSENGER TEST.
HEIGHT TEST
FORCED LANDING TEST.

Instructions for filling in the log book correctly

Flying training began the next day. Roger's first plane was an Avro Lynx J8521 which he flew dual at 1000 feet for 20 minutes with Flight Lieutenant Cox as the Pilot Instructor. Roger flew the straight and level part. He was now a Pilot Officer on probation and progressed eagerly through turns, take off and landings, going up to 3000 feet for spins and how to correct them.

Two of the 503 regular Air Force Instructors. L-r Squadron Leader R D Oxland, Flight Lieutenant Edward I Bussell who was known among the reservists as a somewhat impatient instructor.

On the airfield was a training plane. Roger sat in the cockpit, and when a red warning light came on he would adjust the controls to simulate straight and level flying until the light went off. As his skills increased the lights flashed on faster, sometimes two at once. At the final test all the lights came on at once and a deafening klaxon horn blew shriekingly loud behind the pilot's head. This needed several beers in the officers' mess later on to calm the nerves.

The trainee pilots were enthusiastic and they flew in all but the worst weather. If they could see the trees on the Sleaford road half a mile away they flew. In very strong winds it was fun to fly over Cranwell when they were grounded and do a gleeful circuit or two over the trainees there. Forced landing was often practiced especially in fog, and low level flying in formation for the more advanced pilots was rated as an exhilarating sport.

Roger flew this plane, Avro Lynx J8516, on his second day, dual with Flight Lieutenant Cox, the only instructor to wear glasses.

The Avro was a good plane to handle, usually starting by swinging the propeller. It had one quirk though which meant pilots must wear their goggles at all times as the valves on the Lynx engine had an extra hairspring on the rockers, which occasionally flicked out and back into the pilot's face. One pilot had lost an eye through this.

Flying instruction continued almost daily in the Avro Lynx with a couple of flights in the Fairey Fawn, until Roger completed his first solo flight. The 35 minutes went well, and he progressed towards navigating cross country and beginning the skills of formation flying. When there were a couple of free days he would go home to Cleatham on his motorbike or to his sister Dulcie and her husband Tony, to visit her growing family of little girls, his first and most favourite nieces.

L-r Ursula, Nicola and big sister Jill, little Jo is asleep in the pram

By the end of May Roger had flown 9 hours 45 minutes solo, and 12 hours 5 minutes dual. June 24th Roger celebrated his 21st birthday with a solo flight in the Avro Lynx at 1000 feet to practice landings. On one occasion he had a short flight in a Wapiti to experience a different type of aircraft.

PROGRAMME OF FLYING

MAIN EVENTS

3.00   EVENT 1.

TAKE OFF BY THREE FIGHTER AND THREE DAY BOMBER
SQUADRONS

The following Squadrons will take off :—

Squadron.	Commanding Officer.	Aircraft.	Engine.
No. 3 (Fighter)	Squadron Leader C. A. Stevens, M.C.	Bulldog	Jupiter
No. 17 (Fighter)	Squadron Leader R. Harrison, D.F.C.	Bulldog	Jupiter
No. 54 (Fighter)	Squadron Leader W. E. G. Bryant, M.B.E.	Bulldog	Jupiter
No. 600 (City of London) (Bomber)	Squadron Leader the Rt. Hon. F. E. Guest, C.B.E., D.S.O.	Wapiti	Jupiter
No. 601 (County of London) (Bomber)	Squadron Leader the Rt. Hon. Sir Philip A. G. D. Sassoon, Bart., G.B.E., C.M.G., M.P.	Wapiti	Jupiter
No. 604 (County of Middlesex) (Bomber)	Squadron Leader (Hon. Wing Commander) A. S. W. Dore, D.S.O.	Wapiti	Jupiter

Westland Wapiti. A general purpose aircraft.
Engine : Bristol " Jupiter."

For illustration of Bulldog see page 55.

SEE PAGE 19 FOR SPECIAL ARRANGEMENTS FOR YOUR CONVENIENCE.

Page Thirty-Three

The Westland Wapiti

During August he was into aerobatics. Roger had no problems with
balance or standing on his head, and accustomed to leaning into corners
on his motorbike he did not find it too difficult. By September he was
flying the Fairey Fawn J7189. It was mainly a wooden construction
powered by a Napier Lion 11 or 12 cylinder broad arrow cooled engine.
It sported a forward firing Vickers gun, and a Lewis gun or two which
could be mounted on the Scarff ring which surrounded the rear cockpit.
A normal bomb load of 460 pounds – four 112 lb bombs or two 230 lb

bombs which were carried in racks under the wings. They had camber changing gear operated by a wheel and wheel type aileron control.

The Fairey Fawn with fuel tanks mounted on the wings

Instructor and pupil in Fairey Fawn

On 26th November Sergeant Miles took Roger up to 3000 feet for some aerobatic instruction. The next day he flew himself, aerobatics were something of an ultimate experience.

PROGRAMME OF FLYING—continued.

4.07 EVENT 9.
FLIGHT AEROBATICS

A demonstration of aerobatics by a Flight of No. 43 (Fighter) Squadron, which is equipped with the latest type of Single-seater Fighter.

Pilot.	Aircraft.	Engine.
Flight Lieutenant E. T. CARPENTER, A.F.C.	Fury	Kestrel
Sergeant Pilot S. F. KING	Fury	Kestrel
Sergeant Pilot A. F. UNDERHILL	Fury	Kestrel

For illustration of Fury see page 23.

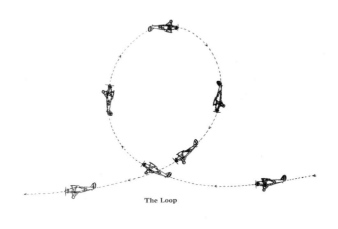

The Loop

SEE PAGE 19 FOR SPECIAL ARRANGEMENTS FOR YOUR CONVENIENCE.

Page Forty-Three

Aerobatic theory

35

Wapitis, Wellingtons and Binderband

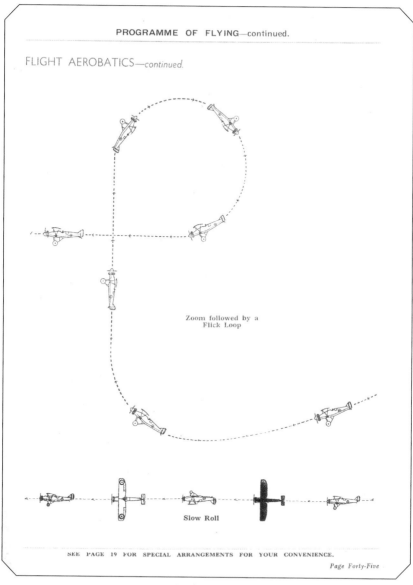

FLIGHT AEROBATICS—*continued.*

Zoom followed by a
Flick Loop

Slow Roll

Aerobatic theory

In spite of being encouraged to fly in all but the worst weathers - safety and instructors permitting - there was not much flying in November, December and January which suited Roger as the Christmas social scene was beckoning at home, and Kirton. There were dances and plays to be produced, and games of mixed hockey after which Roger commented the girls were far too rough.

February 1928 flying was resumed in earnest with longer distance cross-country solos, the course marked in a straight line by pencil on Roger's flying maps. One such cross-country solo included Duxford and Henlow where a Fairey Fawn with a ladder attached had been used for parachute practice.

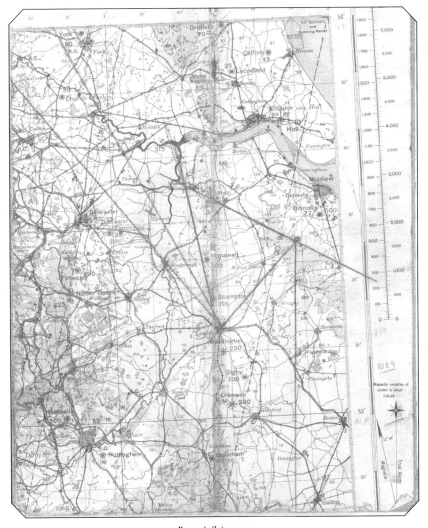

Roger's flying map

April 1st 1928 the prestigious County of Lincoln title was added to 503 Squadron just ten years after the RAF was founded by amalgamating the Royal Flying Corps and the Royal Naval Air Service.

503 Special Reserve County of Lincoln Squadron, 1928. L–r rear Groves, G A Worth, The Hon Francis A J Everleigh de Moleyns, Thompson, J B Brooke, N A Lindley, P Canning. L-r front R H Maw, L V G Barrow, N D Wardrop, D Allison, T H Worth, Morris, Horsfall.

Formation flying, photography, plotting and following compass courses, map reading and using the wireless were all new skills to be mastered. On May 30th 1928 Roger gained his Wings as a Flying Officer, passing the exam with 90% and Distinction. This meant he could wear the winged badge.

In August the reservists began bombing practice using the camera obscura at first, then progressing to three and a half pound practice bombs aimed at a white cross in the centre of the airfield. The stanic chloride contents raising a cloud of 'smoke'. These skills were used to drop a parcel of Roger's dirty washing on the lawn at Cleatham much to Emma and the family's amazement. Mercifully it missed the rose garden, but excellent aerial photos were taken of Cleatham.

Aerial photos of Cleatham (above and overleaf) showing the house and farmyard

Camera obscura - The camera obscura was an early device for the checking of a pilot's ability to fly straight courses, find wind speed and direction, and for the simulation of level bombing. In the roof of the camera obscura was a glass lens through which the image of the aircraft was projected on to a table. The release of an imaginary bomb was indicated by the flash of a magnesium bulb fitted to the aircraft. From

the position of the image in relation to the focal centre and fixed target position on the table, the operator could tell where the bomb would have fallen.

There were two types of camera obscura: a portable type and a fixed type. Because of the mobility of the portable type, it could be used for tactical training exercises during which the bombing of unfamiliar targets could be practised. The fixed camera obscura was a purpose-built structure or part of a multifunctional building, such as the station headquarters at Bicester or the station armoury of the early expansion period. All camera obscuras had to have a clear all-round upward view and were built in a position where they could be seen easily from the air. (British Military Airfield Architecture, p. 166)

Christmastime once again there was little flying so Roger welcomed time at home for parties, the scattered friends enjoying being together again. April 1929 there was no flying so Roger decided to get himself a car. He went by train to the Midlands to the Morgan factory and bought a three-wheeled chassis complete with engine, driving it home perched on a soap box firmly tied on. Some selected friends including the fearless Janett Thornton were allowed to ride with him at this stage.

Gradually he fashioned the body, probably the first three-wheeled saloon car ever made. Sidelights were mounted near the roof, the large single headlight was mounted centrally at the front. There were proper indicators, like little flags, and a removable exhaust baffle for noisy country driving.

Roger's first car

Roger and Janett

41

The completed car

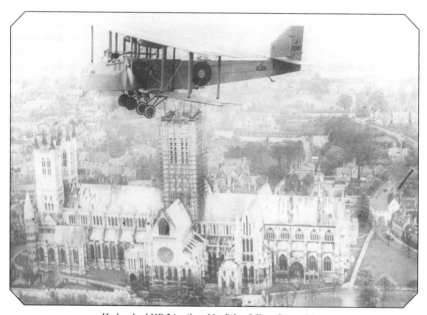

Hyderabad HP 24, piloted by Pilot Officer Roger Maw.

Roger's sister and the little girls loved going out for a picnic. The excitement as they waited by the sitting room window for the first sight of the Aeroplane Car was almost unbearable, and scrambling into the tail of the 'plane' on a rug was ultimate bliss, to be transported to such magical places as Whipsnade Zoo.

May 5th Roger flew a Hyderabad over Lincoln Cathedral when an aerial photo was taken, his log book records he flew with Flying Officers Williams and Morris as passengers. They returned to Waddington to perform a dual forced landing.

The Handley Page Hyderabad was a large twin engine biplane of wooden construction, with Napier Lion water-cooled engines. A noisy aircraft and heavy on the controls weighing 13,535 pounds. It had a range of 693 miles at a true airspeed of 96 miles an hour, with luck and a following wind it could achieve 109 mph. Designed as a night bomber it had several uses. With two crew it was possible to have one as a navigator, photographer, bomb aimer, wireless operator or gunner. Bombing and shooting were practiced regularly. Roger's solo time in the Hyderabad now stood at 28½ hours. In November he practiced a lot of forced landings which were to stand him in good stead throughout his flying life.

Christmas on the airfield was quiet but Roger flew the Hyderabad solo in January and took the forced landing test. One day they flew four times, the first five minutes Flying Officer Cowan was the pilot taking a test. The next three trips of 25 to 45 minutes Roger piloted the Hyderabad and his crew practiced wireless communication, camera and air gunnery, a busy day. There was more instruction on map reading, observing wind speed and direction, vital for accurate navigation. Now the strength of the squadron was ten Regular and nine Reservist officers; a new officers' mess was under construction.

May 1930 they practiced dual night flights and landings. In June Roger and two crew were piloted by Flying Officer Klein to Hendon for Pageant practice. They returned on a compass course cross-country with Roger as second pilot. October was a busy month with some night flying, practice bombing, and cross-country ending with a height test and a war load.

Newall House, the new Officers' Mess, Waddington

Night flying had its exciting moments - the flare path was laid out in a 'T' shape with paraffin flares. The tail was four flares over a distance of 250 yards, the arms ended with flares 100 yards from the head of the 'T', a chilly duty for Paraffin Pete the officer in charge of the flare path. The pilots were meant to land alongside the line of flares, but sometimes landed almost on top giving Paraffin Pete hardly a chance to dive for cover.

December this year was busy with daytime flights and navigation, and target practice for bombs and guns, but Roger did manage a burst of aerobatics for 30 minutes in the Avro Lynx. Christmas was once more a good time to catch up on the farm, family and friends. January he concentrated on navigation, map reading and compass flying and taking another couple of tests. February Roger flew twenty sorties with himself as pilot, more navigation compass courses and cloud flying. There was one blessed 50 minutes of aerobatics with Pilot Officer Carey firmly anchored to the floor by his parachute harness in the rear cockpit. Roger continued photography and progressed to leading formation, more cloud flying, full war load tests and landings, also endurance and petrol consumption tests.

May 17th 1931 Wing Commander Hanmer wrote in Roger's log book, "Qualified 1st Pilot day and night". May brought more formation flying and cross-country for range firing at North Coates on the Lincolnshire coast, some air firing at targets too.

June 1931 flying was all formation and display practice swallowing Roger's birthday when he flew down to Hendon with two crew for the Air

44

Display on June 27th. 503 B Squadron led by their Wing Commander H J Hanmer DFC in the Hyderabads took part in the dramatic big set piece of the display, flying off in neat formation to Waddington.

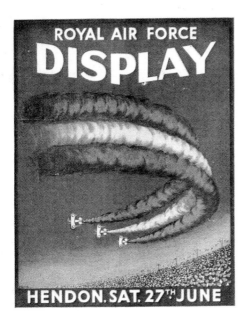

Programme
of the
Royal Air Force
Air Display
1931

PROGRAMME
ONE SHILLING

Cover of display programme

Wapitis, Wellingtons and Binderband

5.19   EVENT 16.

SET PIECE

The Set Piece represents a long-range gun, shelters, ready use ammunition dumps, decauville railway, etc., which have been located in the middle of deserted farm buildings alongside a small wood. War has broken out and the gun has been shelling an important military base, which it threatens to make untenable. The position of the gun has been discovered by sound ranging and air reconnaissance, and as it is apparent that the gun can be reached only by aircraft, a bombing attack is being prepared to destroy it.

The defenders have received information of the intended attack and have allotted two Single-Seater Fighter Squadrons to oppose it. These Squadrons have prepared a temporary landing ground near the gun position; one Squadron is standing by prepared to take off at a moment's notice, and the other is resting. When the event opens the gun is seen in action (for the purpose of this display the rate of fire has been considerably increased). Presently news is received by telephone from advanced observer posts that the attacking Bombers are on their way. The alarm is sounded, the Fighter Squadron which is standing by takes off and the other Fighter Squadron prepares to do the same; the gun, on railway mounting, is withdrawn into the shelter of the wood.

A Squadron of fast Day Bombers is now seen approaching and the defenders' anti-aircraft guns open fire. The Bombers are attacked by the first Fighter Squadron; both sides suffer casualties, but the Bombers succeed in reaching and bombing their objective. They then retire, hotly pursued by the first Fighter Squadron.

Meanwhile a flight of five heavy Bombers appear on the scene and are attacked by the second Fighter Squadron. Casualties occur on both sides, but the Bombers deliver their attack and complete the work of destruction. The ammunition dumps explode and the foundations of the gun are so shaken that it is put out of action.

Squadron.	Commanding Officer.	Aircraft.	Engine.
No. 33 (Bomber)	Squadron Leader W. H. DE W. WALLER, A.F.C.	Hart	Kestrel
No. 503 (Bomber)	Wing Commander, H. I. HANMER, D.F.C.	Hyderabad	Two Lion
No. 41 (Fighter)	Squadron Leader P. HUSKINSON, M.C.	Siskin	Jaguar
No. 56 (Fighter)	Squadron Leader H. V. ROWLEY	Siskin	Jaguar

For illustrations of Hart, Siskin and Hyderabad see pages 49 and 59.

SEE PAGE 19 FOR SPECIAL ARRANGEMENTS FOR YOUR CONVENIENCE.

Page Fifty-Seven

Event 16 Set piece

The young pilots were very interested in the new planes and ideas such as refuelling in the air and the autogyros in the research section.

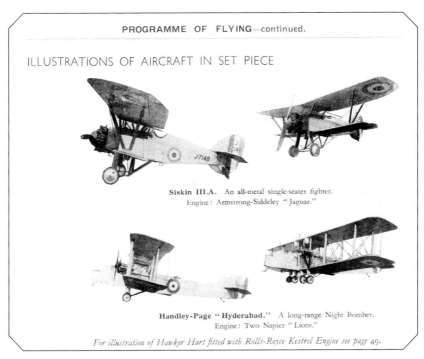

Illustrations of the aircraft in the set piece

Roger continued to fly the Hyderabad with 503 Squadron through July into August when he and his friend Alban Carey were given the opportunity to transfer to the regular RAF. At the interview in the Air Ministry they were asked what squadrons they would like to join. Roger replied "to fly night bombers, and build up my flying hours on multi-engined aircraft, as later on I may be an airline pilot". Alban said he would like to go to the North West Frontier of India for active service in single engine aircraft. They were told that both requests could be arranged. They were, but their names got mixed up and Alban was posted to a night bomber squadron on Boscombe Down, Salisbury Plain while Roger was posted to 39 Squadron on the North West Frontier. They decided to let the postings stand. On leaving Waddington Roger had achieved 363 hours of solo flying and 33 hours dual. His proficiency on the Hyderabad was noted as above average.

At the end of five years of flying together the close knit group of friends had a colossal party in the mess and parted for different destinies.

As luck would have it Roger and Alban's paths were soon to merge again when they were both posted to Boscombe Down where they spent many pleasant off duty times visiting Cheddar Gorge and Wookey Hole, shooting pigeons for farmers in exchange for bacon and egg suppers, and visiting Janett who had moved to Bournemouth now her father had retired.

October 1st 1931 Roger moved to Boscombe Down to join 9B Squadron where he began flying the Vickers Virginia Mk X which was the backbone of the RAF's heavy night bomber force at that time. It had a metal structure covered by fabric and was a rugged reliable twin engine plane, in which Roger learned such vital skills as flying on one engine, and using the Brown S G turn and bank indicator which was electrical and wind driven. The hydraulic brakes and landing lights were an unaccustomed luxury.

Vickers Virginia X J7567. Roger flew this plane the day after he passed his solo by day on V Vs October 16th 1931 – he was not responsible for this forced landing.

He also practiced the Camera gun and navigating when flying as a crew member.

January 1932 Roger moved to Andover to fly the Sidestrand, a twin engine biplane medium day bomber. It was named after a coastal village near to

Boulton and Paul's factory in Norwich where they were built. He found the Sidestrand had good manoeuvrability, excellent for bombing carrying 1050 pounds, and gunnery, having three open defensive positions, nose dorsal and ventral, giving the choice of defence wherever the plane was in the formation. Armament for each position was a 303 inch Lewis gun. The Sidestrand had two 460 hp Bristol Jupiter 9 cylinder air cooled engines giving it speeds of up to 140 mph so it could loop and roll with ease which impressed the spectators at the Hendon Air Displays in mock combats with RAF fighters.

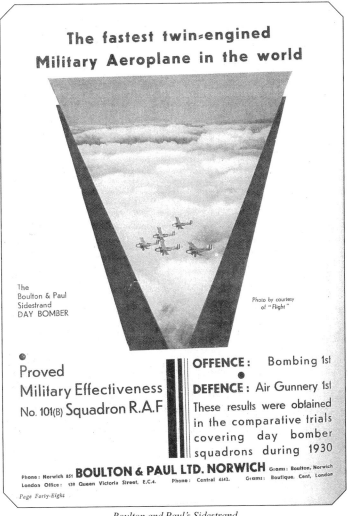

Boulton and Paul's Sidestrand

49

During his stay at Andover there was another letter from Janett, a welcome diversion from the increasing navigation flights, one over his old school Oundle. The Sidestrand could carry three crew as well as the pilot giving Roger plenty of time to practice navigation, map and compass readings when he flew as crew.

Another aircraft Roger mastered on the navigation course was the Tomtit designed as a replacement for the Avro Trainer. It had a steel and duralumin tubular air frame designed by Sidney Camm, chief designer for Hawker. Maximum speed 124 mph. Service ceiling 19,000 feet achieved by an Armstrong Siddeley Mongoose 7 cylinder radial engine. The new blind flying panel was fitted in the cockpit so night flying instruction was possible.

The Hawker Tomtit

April 1932 Roger joined 57B squadron at Netheravon where he flew the Hawker Hart, a single engine two seater biplane, flying solo on his fifth time in the aircraft. The Hawker Hart was designed as a high performance light bomber powered by a Rolls Royce Kestrel 1B 12 cylinder V type engine achieving a speed of 184 mph and a range of over 400 miles. His experience was somewhat varied at Netheravon including a flight in a Kite Balloon recorded in his log as a local flight, airspeed 10 mph.

Hawker Hart. The fastest day bomber in the World.
Engine : Rolls-Royce " Kestrel."

The Hawker Hart

51

The parachute course at Henlow was next, as parachutes were now compulsory for aircrew. Roger and a group of pilots were ushered into a large room with long linoleum covered tables. First there was a short lecture on the sizes of parachute in use for various purposes. The smaller ones with a canvas bag attached carried messages with a small weight. Larger coarse fabric ones were used to drop awkward shaped parcels of ammunition and supplies, and a man sized one to carry about 170 pounds was for aircrew. There were also streamlined containers with their own parachutes attached for dropping certain supplies. Correct folding and packing was essential, so they started on the smaller ones, smoothing out the crumpled canopy and twisted rigging, learning the finer points of parachute care such as hanging to dry for forty eight hours after each drop. Ideally they would be repaired and repacked every two months, and drop tested from 1000 feet once a year.

The packing was the easy part. Outside on the airfield was an old biplane bomber, a Vickers Vimy with a small platform attached far out on the lower wing. The trainee parachutist stood on the platform facing backwards pressed against the strut by the slipstream – just holding on. The old Vimy lumbered into the sky, circled back across the airfield into wind at about 800 feet. The pilot signalled with his hand and the parachutist edged round the strut hanging on grimly with the left hand – the right clamped nervously to the handle of the parachute rip cord. At the second signal he pulled the rip cord handle hard and BANG he was torn from the platform and floating quietly in the air. The perfect landing was to twist downwind, bend the knees and roll over on impact. The ambulance, well equipped with splints was never far away from the white circle that was the parachutists goal. Roger did his training but seeing several people break their legs he refused to jump saying that if he needed to bail out, when the time came he knew what to do.

News came through of Roger's posting to India, where he would be for four years, so there was some leave allowed and many friends and family gathered at Cleatham to wish him well.

Vickers Vimy

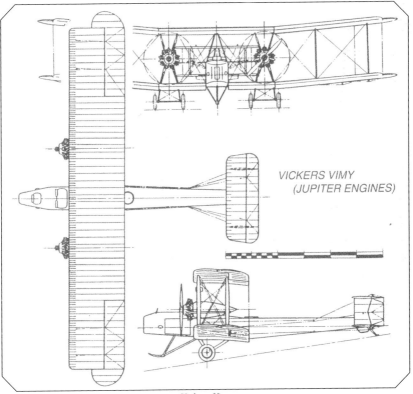

VICKERS VIMY
(JUPITER ENGINES)

Vickers Vimy

4.15   EVENT 10.

PARACHUTE EVENT

This event is a demonstration by the Parachute Section of the Home Aircraft Depôt of the parachutes which are used in the Royal Air Force. The method demonstrated will be that employed in normal training. The Parachutists stand on the wings of the aeroplane and at a given signal pull the release handle. After the parachute has opened the Parachutist is "pulled off" the aircraft. It will be realised that in a strong wind the Parachutist is travelling fast over the ground and the landing may be sufficiently heavy to cause minor injuries. Unless, therefore, weather conditions are entirely satisfactory for this demonstration, "live" descents will be abandoned, and dummies will be dropped from the aircraft.

Aircraft.	Engines.
Vimy	Jupiter

Parachutists.

Flight Lieutenant J. B. LYNCH	Leading Aircraftsman H. HUDSON
Sergeant C. MAYHEW	Leading Aircraftsman J. HUBBARD
Corporal H. MARSHALL	Aircraftsman S. C. ROONEY

Vickers Vimy

Famous as the British aircraft which carried out the first direct Atlantic flight in 1919. Now used for training purposes.

SEE PAGE 19 FOR SPECIAL ARRANGEMENTS FOR YOUR CONVENIENCE.

Page Forty-Seven

Pic 24c Parachute event at Hendon RAF Air Display

October 10th 1932 Roger hired a Gipsy Moth G ABKL, a two seater biplane, a slightly later model than the Tiger Moth with the engine higher up which gave it a more streamlined look. Together with Flying Officer Finney they made the flight from Reading to Sherbourne to visit Janett Thornton and Vi Garvey who were working as waitresses in the Three Wishes cafe. Roger flew Janett for her first flight, which he recorded in the log book as local flying at Sherbourne. It was a fitting farewell as he was off to India to patrol the Northwest Frontier, joining his ship the next day.

Gipsy Moth

—OVER THE HORIZON—

Roger and friend ready for adventure

The troop ship HMT Lancaster lay alongside the dock at Southampton. Scores of Army and RAF men and porters scurrying up the many gangways. Waiting for Roger in the cramped cabin he would share with three other junior officers was a nice surprise, a telegram from Janett Thornton and Vi Garvey.

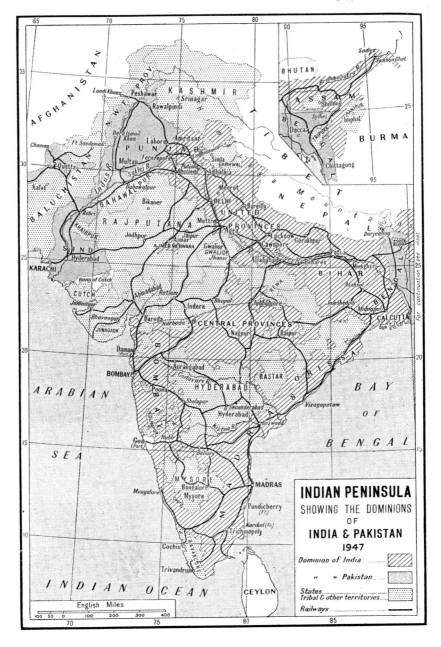

INDIAN PENINSULA
SHOWING THE DOMINIONS
OF
INDIA & PAKISTAN
1947

Dominion of India
"   " Pakistan
States
Tribal & other territories
Railways

HMT Lancaster

Life on board was crowded and very formal, uniform being worn in the day and mess kit in the evenings.

Bill Coulson and Bud on rail, self in deckchair stretching

After the Bay of Biscay the dining rooms and bars resumed a brisk trade. The colour smell and noisy bustle of Port Said provided a welcome break in the journey. Roger saw beggars for the first time, even children holding out eager hands for coins.

Eventually they were through the Suez Canal and round the Persian Gulf to Basra to drop off some RAF personnel and collect others to go on to India. The ship steamed past Aden, across the Arabian Sea to Karachi. With gin at two pence (2d) a tot it was easy in the bright sunshine to look forward confidently to flying over the Northwest Frontier.

As the ship docked some senior RAF officers came on board to give the pilots and aircrew their destinations. Roger's posting was to Risalpur, a Northwest Frontier station equipped with Hawker Harts. "Your Bearers are waiting on the quay, and they will show you where to go, and see to your luggage." A young Indian neatly dressed wearing a khaki turban came towards the gangway. "Maw sahib?" Roger nodded. "Salaam sahib, I am your bearer Ibraham Khan. I am sent down from the Officers' Mess at Risalpur to be your personal servant. Your bistra here sahib." He pointed to a bundle of green canvas sprouting wooden sticks, which turned out to be a sort of glorified bed roll complete with mattress, sheet and pillow. Everywhere Roger went for the next four years would provide a charpoy, a bed frame strung with jute cord on which to lay his bistra. It also contained a canvas wash basin with folding stand, a canvas bucket and a small bath.

Ibraham

59

The troop train lay dusty and silent beside the quay. Ibraham escorted Roger to the compartment he would share with three other officers. There seemed to be three classes on the train, Officers, Troops, and Bearers with other servants, enough to keep the dining cars busy when they stopped for meals. There was enough time to go to one or two shops and buy films for the camera and a Bombay Bowler to keep his head protected from the sun.

At last the engine steamed up complete with cowcatcher and mournful bell and they began the journey, four days and three nights puffing across the endless dusty plains of the Sind Desert, stopping only for meals when everyone piled out onto the trackside and walked to the dining cars.

One of the many rail bridges

During the long journey there was plenty of time for conversation and exchanging information between the pilots. It seemed their destinies were arranged by the Aircraft Depot at Karachi, who loaned them out to the Indian Government. The Indian Government paid the RAF personnel, and provided for all their requirements during their stay in India. The Aircraft Depot held, stored, repaired and distributed all the aircraft and equipment on behalf of the Indian Government. A Pilot Officer's wage was about 400 rupees a month (£36) which was a little more than the home rate of pay. Roger's bearer Ibraham would cost him

Thelum railway station en route to Lahore

26 rupees a month (about £2), but he was worth his weight in gold when it came to arranging things with the local tradesmen. Urdu was the main language locally so Roger and Ibraham conversed in a mixture of both, each picking up words from the other.

At each stop Ibraham would appear and tidy up the compartment, making up the beds in the evening, and organising the sweeper to clean the carriage and empty the thunderbox. The meals were curry, not Roger's favourite, but at every station the platform was full of food sellers and beggars. The RAF had been strictly warned to avoid these sticky fly covered sweetmeats, but the fruit looked appetising, here Ibraham came to the rescue with the potassium permanganate crystals he had been trained to carry, mixing them with water to make 'Pinky Parni', a solution to wash the fruit, some of which the Englishmen had never seen, but they were keen to try a different flavour to curry.

As the train snailed north the temperature dropped and the scenery began to change, giving the men a chance to cover their pale knees, exchanging regulation khaki shorts for their blue uniform worn on the frontier stations for the few cooler months. The desert gave way to the Punjab, a fertile province just below the Himalayan foothills. The train crossed the mighty Indus River which marked the border between the Punjab and the North West Frontier.

Peshawar, the final destination of the train, lies a few miles from the entrance to the Khyber Pass which leads through to Afghanistan. For the weary travellers the ancient teeming city with its tree-lined streets was a welcome sight after the endless dusty plains. Fleets of three ton lorries, Crossleys, drew up to take the pilots and airmen to their final destinations, Kohat, Peshawar aerodrome and Risalpur.

The Crossley

Roger's journey was along well defined roads with many tribesmen walking along in the middle. It seemed that the British government had guaranteed the safety of all travellers within three feet of the road from the continual feuding in this tribal territory, so every man carried a rifle. Many of these were made at the Kohat Rifle Factory where they used any steel, even old railway lines with great skill. Using only hand tools good usable rifles were produced.

The thirty miles to Risalpur were dusty and crowded as it was the main road from the frontier province into the Punjab and central India with the Northwest railway running beside it. At Nowshera, a garrison town, the Crossleys turned north towards the foothills of the Himalays. The journey ended in a green oasis of wide grass edged roads lined with square brick bungalows, each having its own garden.

Frontier tribesmen

Ibraham was quick to find Roger's bungalow and install his bistra and luggage. There was a wide veranda on each side of the bungalows for maximum shade. Four pilots shared the bungalow, each having his own bedroom, sitting room and bathroom. The bath water emptied out of a hole in the wall into the garden, the only downside being that scorpions, tarantulas and the occasional snake had easy access. Huge clanking fans were the only way of cooling the inside temperature down from the

63

summer 127 degrees in the shade, and many of the RAF personnel slept outside at night on the veranda, or in the garden.

Each bungalow was managed on a community basis by the bearers who lived out at the back a little distance away. They organised the mali gardener, dhobi laundryman, a sweeper to do the cleaning, and a chowkidar watchman who prowled about the bungalow at nights. Hair cuts could also be arranged.

My barber

The mess was nearby with a large shady garden, tennis courts and a swimming pool. There was no Officers club which Roger would have expected as Risalpur had two cavalry regiments as well as the large RAF station but as the wives and girlfriends were free to use the pool, tennis and squash courts in the day time there was a more friendly less formal atmosphere. The lack of a golf course was easily overcome by driving to Nowshera for 6 a.m. tee off on holiday days and back to the mess for breakfast at nine.

The first day was spent in reporting officially to the Adjutant, reading standing orders, and meeting the Station Commander with the other officers of 11 and 39 squadrons. The formalities over the new pilots made their way to the hangar where the Hawker Harts were being wheeled in at one o'clock after the day's flying was completed. There they met the Flight Sergeants and their men who serviced and kept the planes running, their expertise was a valuable mine of information. Flying began early, 6 a.m. as the afternoon's heat and dust became too much. This gave the riggers and fitters time to refuel and repair before the next day.

Roger had flown Harts with 57 Squadron at Netheravon in the previous summer, achieving nearly 20 hours solo, so he was familiar with many of its characteristics. The top speed of 184 mph was produced by the Rolls Royce Kestrel engine, cooled by ethylene glycol through a radiator which was wound in and out by hand according to the temperature on the gauge. The liquid cooling meant the engine was closely cowled giving a streamlined sporty look. The new pilots were soon to find the balancing act of adjusting the radiator to the correct temperature, a skilled and dangerous business. The wheel brakes were also very tricky, pneumatically operated, one or both would sometimes jam and tip the plane on its nose or swing sideways. Of the few instruments the Harts possessed the altimeter was the most important.

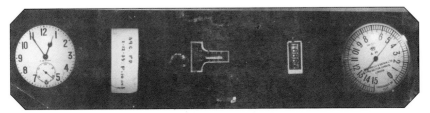

The altimeter on the right was made in Hatton Garden!

Roger and the new pilots were given a few days to acclimatise to their surroundings before beginning flying duties. The Station Commander made it clear this would be essential work policing the Empire, observing the movements of the natives, and dropping supplies to the more remote camps.

The social life at the RAF stations followed closely the Army's somewhat Victorian protocol. Each Officer was expected to have calling cards engraved with his name, Roger H Maw Royal Air Force. The rank of

Pilot Officer was not mentioned, later on in the distant future when he achieved Flight Lieutenant this could be added. To leave his cards with the Station, Squadron and Flight Commanders the married officers, Chief of Police, Magistrates, Important Civilians and the Regiments of the Risalpur Brigade, Roger had to wear a light suit with collar and tie. The job was speeded up by the second-hand bicycle acquired for him by Ibraham. This would bring him many invitations to dinner and parties. Leaving his card in the Regimental mess a little later in the day meant he might meet an army officer going into the bar and be invited to join him for a drink, a welcome relief from the dust and heat outside.

The Squadron Leader and other officers would occasionally throw a drinks party for the unmarried officers so they could get to know each other better and meet some young ladies. Roger soon discovered the Sunday tradition of Curry Tiffin at the Peshawar Club, a great meeting place for friends over Murree beer, Gin Slings, and Tom Collins with the regimental band playing Ain't Misbehavin in the background. The Tiffin had many delicacies besides curry which pleased Roger. The young ladies were mostly from the 'Fishing Fleet'. They had come to India, heavily chaperoned on the boat, to stay with relations and improve their knowledge of the Empire. Some were looking for husbands, but many just wanted an occasional escort for dancing or tennis and riding.

Roger's first flights were as a passenger with a spot of dual flying which ended with the Hart swinging after landing reminding him of a previous landing at Netheravon when his log book recorded "swung and broke the aircraft".

Roger soon began flying himself with LAC Hogan for company and much needed local and technical advice. On good days the foothills of the Himalayas were clearly visible to the north, gigantic snow capped peaks, among them Everest. Venturing further flying up to two hours at a time, and making local landings at places that Rudyard Kipling would have known, Rawalpindi, Kushalgarh, Arawali, and Miramashar. Landings were practiced over and over again on the hard sun baked ground. There were several small emergency landing grounds scattered over the vast territory, each with some fuel and water.

The last flight in December was on the 10th so as there were ten days holiday before Christmas Roger and fellow pilots Jack Atkins and Pat Moncton decided to have a shooting expedition for a few days. Their bearers were good at putting a local shooting trip together for the high flying quail and snipe. They loaded an ancient tourer with bistras and warm clothes for the chilly nights, a gramophone and other essentials.

Transport for three sahibs and luggage

The road to the shoot was interesting, including a bridge of boats with a string of well loaded camels crossing.

Loaded camels

67

Loaded camels and boat bridge

Roam Shah the chiliare, gamekeeper supplied a boat for accommodation, with a cook, and a colourful collection of beaters.

Roam Shah, our chiliare

Some of the beaters

Some of the beaters

The bistras were much in use, the friends taking photos of each other, which must have impressed any Hindus as they seemed to regard washing as part of their religion.

Wapitis, Wellingtons and Binderband

Jack washing   *Roger in the bath*

The shooting trip was a great success with enthusiastic beaters and a good keeper. Accommodation on the boat was adequate, and the cook managed a good supply of food from the small fire on the foredeck of the boat, and much needed tiffin for breaks between shooting in the morning and afternoon. The gramophone was much enjoyed by beaters and the shooting party.

The boat

A stop for tiffin

The gramophone party

The second day's bag of game with our cook on right, the chiliare,
keeper in the middle and Culler a bearer.

Christmas brought a lot of letters and parcels which had taken seven weeks to arrive, one of the letters was from Janett. Any homesickness was swiftly drowned in Murree Beer. The usual Christmas fare of turkey and plum pudding were served. Trees were sent down from the Hill Depot and the barrack blocks were decorated in competition with each other. There was no flying so a good time was had by all.

After the festivities it was good to get back to some flying duties, patrolling the vast area of the Northwest Frontier, watching out for any unusual gatherings of natives in the foothills and passes. From time to time tribal feuds would spill over into small wars. Some villages supported the British Empire in return for their protection, and when these villages came under attack they would send word to the nearest Regiment. The RAF would then fly over the offending village, dropping leaflets in the local language, saying bombing would commence that afternoon, so every native took his family and livestock up the hill, a good distance away to wait until the bombers came. A few shots were fired at the planes and they returned to rebuild and continue their dislike of the British. These journeys were fraught with difficulties for the Harts, visibility was one, and a lack of reliable maps was another, as many of the rivers and hills looked alike in the blinding sun. Sandstorms were another danger for the pilots in the open cockpits and their engines. It was so very different from the solid reliable green country of Lincolnshire that Roger knew so well.

There were some notorious tribal leaders such as the Faqir of Ipi who was well known for inciting troubles and at times lived in caves that neither the Army nor the RAF had ever managed to locate or destroy.

Roger and his squadron took part in regular demonstration flights over the northern territories, beyond Peshawar northwards into the Khyber and other passes up to the foothills of the Himalayas, home to the Mohmand tribes, over deep gorges, through the territory of The Wali of Swat, seeing the tops of the highest peaks towards Chinese Turkestan, the roof of the World. Peaks exceeding 20,000 feet where flying access could only be along the narrow gorges of the Indus and its tributaries and very dangerous. Regular flights were never made in the very high country.

Climbing the Laorai Pass, the entrance to Chitral. Kohistan on the right.
Afghanistan away to the left.

There was one plane that iced up badly in this area and crash landed upside down in six feet of snow. The pilot and his gunner survived and were rescued by The Wali of Swat's men. They were given up for dead by the RAF at Risalpur, but astounded everyone by eventually making their way back to the station having been looked after personally by The Wali.

Flying in spring was inspiring, views of snow capped mountains ahead in the gin clear air, and glimpses of tumbling churning snow-melted waters in the deep gorges below, sacred waters feeding sacred rivers.

Navigation was not very easy due to the inaccuracy of the few maps available, but where railway lines crossed the plains it was simpler, although one pilot did actually follow the north south railway instead of the east west, no, he never lived it down. A favourite game with pilots was to fly beside a train just a little slower giving the impression they were flying backwards to the amazement of the driver and passengers.

British engine hauls a passenger train.

Frontier mail train on a curve.

February 1933 Roger's squadron did quite a bit of formation flying, gun practice, camera gun and air to air firing. Formation flying was used on patrol over the Mohmand territory.

Patrolling in formation between the clouds

Communication from plane to plane, and plane to ground needed some new skills. Zogging was a form of morse code used by pilots from their open cockpits with a long arm sweeping down with closed fist equalled a dash, and a short downward sweep from the elbow a dot. Slow but effective, many messages, serious or rude were exchanged in the sky. The Popham Panel was a standard way of communicating from the ground to the pilot above. It consisted of a panel, or blanket laid on the ground with symbols on it, straight lines, arrows and circles. Each plane had a book to 'read' the code, if the code requested any supplies carried by the plane they could be dropped straight away. Most of the army foot patrols also carried a basket of pigeons, so communication was possible.

Practice on the firing range was a standard exercise with the pilots flying from Risalpur to the range north of Peshawar. Roger took off at 6.15 a.m. with all guns loaded, dived at the square canvas targets firing his Vickers guns till he ran out of ammunition, then he turned and flew low level along the line so his gunner had several chances to use his ammunition. Exactly an hour later they landed back at Risalpur and handed the plane to another pilot and gunner. When it was his turn as Safety Officer Roger had to stay overnight at Peshawar, get up at 5.30 a.m. and go by lorry to the firing range to manage it for the day, recording scores, patching up targets, and cooking tinned steak and tinned sausages to pass the time with his men.

Roger flew on several occasions with Leading Aircraftman Albert Simpson and they got on well together, Albert appreciating Roger's sense of humour and his endless supply of funny stories. His duties as a Leading Aircraftman were many and varied, including morse code, photography, maintaining and occasionally flying the Harts. He always knew where he had stowed the Popham Panel book in the rear cockpit. The small parachutes for dropping messages, the ammunition for the gun, the chitty to give to hostile tribesmen promising them a lot of money if they returned the pilots unharmed to the RAF station in case of crash landing were all safely packed in there too. Albert also made sure the flask had hot coffee in and a wicker basket containing a spot of tiffin. Flights with Albert were good. One night they 'borrowed' a plane to fly to a local town for a party. Albert has memories of Roger standing on his head in one corner of the bar with a pint of beer beside him. It was a good party and they barely remembered flying home. Albert shared

Roger's dislike of the intense heat and was amused to see him land and open a brightly coloured parasol open over his head as he taxied to the shade of the hangar. Roger was inventive too. When this plane landed badly there were no spare wheels so he took a couple off a battery trolley as the axles were the same so it could be wheeled to the hangar for the rest of the repairs.

A group photo was taken of 39b Squadron, Risalpur in October 1935 when Roger was away at the Aircraft Park in Lahore. Albert Simpson is sitting cross legged second from left in front row.

In July Roger teamed up with Flight Lieutenant Whitley to fly down to the Aircraft Park at Lahore to make tests on some of the planes there. The Aircraft Park was the centre for the Heavy Transport flight, troop carriers, the Vickers Victoria, Valencia, Hinaidi and Clive among them. The first tests were climbing trials on the Vickers Victoria, as Roger had flown a Vickers Virginia previously he was accustomed to the size of the aircraft. They made several local flights for a couple of hours carrying various weights to 5000 feet, always with four crew. Then they made a five and a half hour flight to Quetta up to 7000 feet, several local flights there for vital cross-country and consumption tests, returning to Lahore via Montgomery.

"We are testing the Vickers Victoria v1 K2340 at Lahore and Quetta for the Indian Government, June 29ᵗʰ 1933."

The next plane Roger flew with Pilot Officer Raynham was the Hinaidi J 7747 which had quite a history. The young pilots took the Hinaidi up a couple of times, short flights to test it. Landing a Hinaidi was a fine art especially in windy conditions, with no brakes and a soup plate shaped tail skid anything could and occasionally did happen.

J7745 at Peshawar in January 1929 during the relief of the British Legation at Kabul.
(*M.O.D.—Crown Copyright*)

The original Hinaidi J7745, doped aluminium for tropical service, was used as the personal transport of Sir Philip Sassoon during his official tour of RAF stations in India, while Under Secretary of State for Air; thereafter it served till 1934 alongside the Clive IIs with the RAF Heavy Transport Flight at Lahore, where it had been based since sharing with No.70 Squadron's Vickers Victorias the evacuation of civilians from the beleaguered British Embassy at Kabul during the rebellion against King Amanullah of Afghanistan in December 1928. This operation was completed on 25 February, 1929, after 586 passengers had been air-lifted in 82 flights over the 10,000 ft mountains to Peshawar, without a single casualty during very severe winter conditions. J7745's contribution comprised eight flights to Kabul and back, carrying 38 passengers and five tons of their baggage; Flt Lieut Anderson had flown it at short notice to Peshawar from Hinaidi near Baghdad in one of the longest overland ferry flights carried out by the RAF at that date; as J7745 was not equipped for night flying, a hurricane lamp had to be used to illuminate the pilot's instruments for landing after dark.

206

The Clive was next, it could carry 17 troops, tests were made with and without full bomb load.

Clive. J 9948 Supply dropping. Note the bombs.

"OK who's flying this thing?"

August was a busy month of shorter flights. Each day starting at 6 a.m. with the staccato spit and crackle from the stub exhaust pipes along each side of the engine cowling of the Harts, the exhilaration of a swift take off and momentary peace before the business of the day, practice bombing, air firing, and several 'bombing' practices on the camera obscura with Leading Aircraftman (LAC) Albert Simpson.

During September Roger and Albert did quite a lot of aerial photography.

The annual bombing exercises at Kohat were an opportunity for the Risalpur pilots to see some new country and make new friends. They flew over a mountain range sliced by deep gorges noticing the Kohat pass below with its clearly defined road snaking through it. A small green oasis appeared and the Harts descended to the sun baked square of aerodrome which was surrounded by barbed wire with searchlights. The perimeter fences had been put up in 1923 when a young girl Mollie Ellis was abducted from her parents bungalow by Afridi Tribesmen, later returned mercifully unharmed.

Roger and Albert climbed out of the plane to be greeted by their Kohat hosts, and shown to their quarters. The Officers' Mess was a low single storey building with a pleasant garden, but the single officers quarters were in a two storey block and not as spacious as the bungalows at Risalpur.

Kohat had a civilian cinema in the Bazaar area. It was quite an experience. Outside the cinema was a collection of homemade rifles, neatly stacked by the many tribesmen some of whom had walked miles to see the silent film. As they regarded the British as their protectors they were happy to leave their weapons outside. Roger's one rupee ticket allowed him inside onto the balcony with officers in mess kit and memsahibs in evening dress. The centre section held British soldiers, airmen and Indians, then a barbed wire entanglement, and beyond this the four anna seats were occupied cheerfully and noisily by the hawking, spitting tribesmen as they chewed beetlenut.

Kohat had a gymkhana club overlooking the polo ground. There were tennis courts and a nine hole golf course nearby, which resulted in some interesting moments, golf balls through the polo posts or a polo puck swiftly followed by horse and rider on one of the greens.

A Frontier tribesman

The Kohat squadrons had Wapitis, a two seater biplane with wings of equal length powered by a 480 hp Bristol Jupiter 9 cylinder radial engine, which was started either by perching precariously on the lower wing and winding away at low geared starting handles or the bag and rope technique. The canvas bag was fitted over the tip of the propeller, attached to this was twenty feet of rope and two strong airmen who rushed away at speed, falling in a heap when the engine finally fired. Roger soon found this was no dual control aircraft as the rear cockpit was designed for a standing gunner, his harness clipped to the floor, surrounded by a rotatable Scarff ring onto which he clipped his guns, there was a small flap down seat for calmer moments. He had an emergency stick that could be plugged into the flying controls as they passed through the rear cockpit allowing a competent airman to land the plane in an emergency. Communication was by a simple rubber speaking tube between the open cockpits. There was a good deal of banter between the Wapiti and Hart pilots, and the two weeks of bombing practice passed quickly.

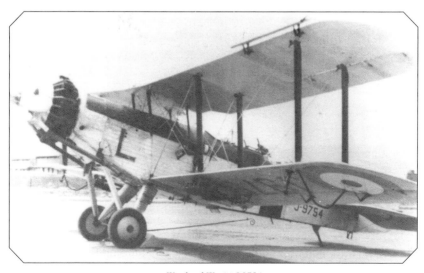

Westland Wapiti J 9754

Roger's next posting was to the Aircraft Park at Lahore where he had previously tested several of the larger planes. He flew a Vickers Victoria to Quetta for various tests spending several days there, before returning to Lahore.

June 3rd 1935 the commanding Officer of the Aircraft Park called all the pilots and airmen together to tell them the shocking news of the huge earthquake at Quetta. Roger and Whitley lost no time in setting off in the Vickers Victoria K 2340 with three crew, four passengers who were likely to help at Quetta and all the medical supplies they could. They flew first to Multan to refuel and take on drinking water knowing these would be in short supply.

As they approached the airfield they saw a huge swirling yellow cloud of dust miles wide and hundreds of feet high, visibility was very bad, even in their open cockpit. Roger was glad he had spent so much time at Quetta recently so he knew the angle of approach for the airfield, but he was horrified to see a great crack had opened up in the main landing area, canvas strips on the ground indicated the safer landing areas. There were several smaller planes parked up, Roger noticed the Wapitis from Kohat had already arrived with medical support from their local hospital. It was a roughish landing and the bandaged airman who limped over to help them park broke the awful news of barrack blocks collapsing. The heavy concrete roofs had crashed down on sleeping airmen, many of whom were killed. Everyone not on essential duties seemed to be digging people and vital equipment out of the rubble and dust.

The aircraft hangars appeared to be alright as Roger and Whitley peered through gaps in the twisted metal doors, but inside the Wapitis of two squadrons had slithered and collided on the heaving floors until only three planes out of the 24 appeared serviceable, and some were obviously a write off. The pilots of the smaller planes stayed only long enough to eat their sandwiches and refuel their planes, which they did themselves before taking off to return to Kohat, Ambala and Lahore, hopefully before dark, as some of the older planes had to light a stable lantern in the cockpit to see the altimeter. Roger and Whitley stayed the night, sleeping as best they could after helping with the digging, and refuelling the Victoria.

Quetta was divided by a valley, the Durrane Nullah, with the First Indian Division and Army Staff College virtually untouched on the north side, but the native city and the RAF station to the south devastated. Next day they took off to do some aerial photography, Roger and Whitley were horrified to see the Native City as the yellow dust clouds eased back, there did not appear to be one building left standing, and tiny figures digging desperately and, still white bundles gathered in silent rows.

Earthquake at Quetta

The army sent in tanks to help clear the rubble

Digging for survivors

Time for a spot of tiffin - a break in a long flight, Roger is on the right

QUETTA EARTHQUAKE
AREA
Neg. Nos. 07255-07294
11:00 Hrs. 4.6.35.
7 Inch. 11000 Ft a.s.l.
Scale 1 : 287 ½s. approx.

Before the earthquake

After the earthquake

The official toll was 55 RAF personnel and dependants and 66 local employees killed. In Quetta City it was estimated that 15,000 people died.

From June 3rd until 21st Roger and Whitley flew the Victoria to and from Quetta to Lahore, Karachi, Reti, Peshawar and Fort Sandeman, a total of almost 102 hours in three weeks carrying 154 passengers. Several of the longer flights included some night flying.

There was a short break of a few days before the Victoria was wheeled out again for Roger and Whitley to fly the Air Officer Commanding, Air Marshal Sir Ludlow Hewitt and passengers on a tour which included Ambala, Multan, Quetta, Karachi and Sukor returning to Lahore by Multan and Ambala.

AOCs tour Roger climbing into his pilots seat at front

Roger's next entry in his log book was "No flying for 3 months owing to leave and Hill Depot."

The RAF had built a Hill Depot at Lower Topa in the Murree hills 7,000 feet above sea level. The huts were on the hillside among the pine trees, and only five miles from the civilian hill station at Murree, which also had the famous brewery. Every airman had two months a year here between May and October. Most of the junior officers could afford some time in the hills, and some led parties of airmen to Lower Topa where there was a leisurely routine with plenty of time for sports after acclimatising to the altitude. By June the temperature was over 100 degrees Fahrenheit in the shade so a break from the intense heat was very welcome.

Ibraham and the other bearers loaded bistras, luggage and iceboxes of beer into the waiting Crossleys, heavy duty lorries. Roger and the other pilots and airmen and bearers climbed in for the long dusty ride, the road running straight from Peshawar to Rawalpindi crossing the Indus half way at Attock where road and rail share the same bridge. At midday Ibraham and the other bearers unpacked the Murree beer which was swiftly drunk in the blazing sun accompanied by sandwiches and several small boys hoping for a handout.

Rawalpindi appeared dusty and neglected, but the low smudge on the northern horizon was encouraging, and soon some of the higher peaks were visible, still snow capped over by Kashmir, the ranges of hills leading to the great peaks of Everest, Rakaposhi, and Harmosh 29,000 feet or more.

Then began the epic climb of 5000 feet in 35 miles. A superbly engineered road consisting of hairpin bends clinging to sheer cliff faces. As the temperature dropped the scent of pine trees drifted through the open canvas sides. When they arrived the bearers settled their pilots in their new quarters and Roger had a pleasant surprise, another letter from Janett.

The winding gear

Ten Green Bottles

Life at Lower Topa, was relaxed with time for riding and making friends, writing letters, drinking beer and enjoying life.

*Roger continued his hobby of making model planes, this was quite a big one with an elastic 'engine'
which he wound up by turning the propeller several hundred times using the simple wheel and
handle attached to a chair arm. His comment on one of the pictures of it flying "You might think
this was real!"*

Janett's letter was answered and several more written home to Cleatham, the Garveys and Roger's brothers and sister always sending love to his four nieces Jill, Ursula, Nic and little Jo.

Roger with the plane and friends

Roger also continued to increase his skill standing on his head much to the amusement of the assembled company.

Standing on his head

96

With the change of climate appetites returned, and a good night's sleep under a blanket away from the clanking fans was so good.

At the end of his stay Roger was happy to return to flying duties at the Aircraft Park in Lahore where he flew a Valentia, a plane he became increasingly fond of flying.

Vickers Valentia. The pilot's open cockpit is well forward of the engines.

Roger's next mission in the Valentia was to collect Colonel Erskine from Gilgit and fly him to Peshawar. Gilgit was the most northerly point of British India among some of the highest peaks in the Himalays, situated on the camel route from Chinese Turkestan through incredibly narrow passes and tracks down to the Indian Plains where they sold their carpets and rugs. Roger's co pilot was Flt Lt Downs, they had a crew of three, all eager to see Gilgit as they had heard so much about it.

They took off at 6 a.m. after checking the engines carefully and flew to Chakala where they refuelled and filled the empty two gallon jerry cans as there was no petrol at Gilgit.

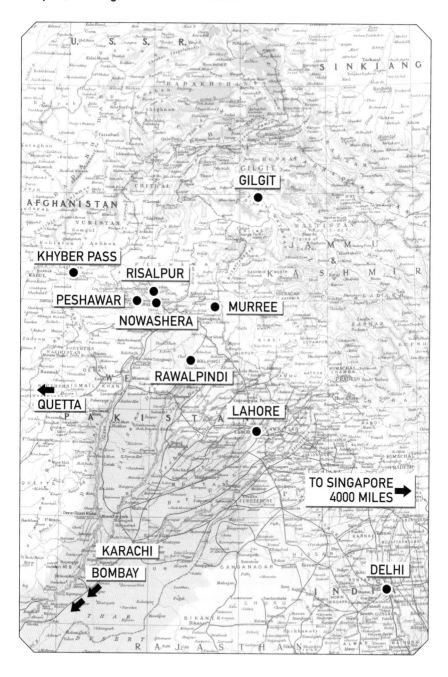

GILGIT

KHYBER PASS

RISALPUR

PESHAWAR

NOWASHERA

MURREE

RAWALPINDI

QUETTA

LAHORE

TO SINGAPORE
4000 MILES

KARACHI

BOMBAY

DELHI

Refuelling

The weather was good as they flew north up the Indus River into a deepening gorge, further into the foothills of the Himalayas. Roger kept the plane at a steady 1300 feet, one glance down showed the dark tumbling waters freed from the melting snows carving their way through sheer rock face below. High mountains loomed above and it was essential to keep a steady course, but almost impossible when someone spotted Everest way to the left with its tell tale plume of snow blowing off the summit.

Nanga Parbat reared up 26,620 feet seeming nearer than 22 miles away.

The pilots watched closely for any clouds forming around the peaks, among them Harmosh 24,720 feet high. The river veered north east and after almost three hours they spotted the Gilgit landing strip on a high vee shaped plateau between the Indus and one of its tributaries. There were two 'runways' forming a cross, three ending in a sheer drop down, and one ending in a steep hillside up. As the windsock hung limp Roger

Nanga Parbat,

Gilgit flight, October 17th 1932

chose to go in facing the hill, carefully and slowly as he dared he put the big plane down, it stopped just short of the hill. A small party of Indians on ponies came down from a rough stony track where they had held back to wait for the engines to stop. Mr Clarke the British resident had ridden down to meet them. "Nice landing, welcome to Gilgit." Mr Clarke's men helped to secure the Valentia to the hard stony ground with strong screw-in stakes and rope, covered the engines, and refuelled the tanks through a funnel and chamois leather filter.

They rode up the steep track for an hour until the ground levelled out to a small well-cultivated area surrounding a huddle of huts and houses with an old fort flying the Union Jack. They spent a very sociable evening with Mr Clarke and Colonel Erskine, learning that Marco Polo had played the famous polo game here on the agile hill ponies, and the Gilgit men still played it. After a cool comfortable night lulled to sleep by the roaring Indus below they returned to the plane, double checked everything, and took off at full throttle into the steep dark gorge, sun rising over the great Himalayan peaks, an awesome sight. Three hours and 20 minutes later they landed at Peshawar to find they had been 'officially missing' for 24 hours with no one unduly worried as radio contact was rarely possible in the mountains. Leaving Mr Clarke's shopping list with the Adjutant so he could inform the next camel caravan which plodded up to Gilgit every six months to deliver essential supplies. Roger and Downs returned to Lahore that afternoon.

The next mission for Roger, Whitley and the Valentia was to take the General Officer Commanding (GOC) West and two officials on a tour to Quetta via Karachi. The flight to Karachi took six and a half hours where they stayed the night. Karachi to Quetta was just over four hours so the GOC had plenty of time to inspect the earthquake damage and discuss plans for rebuilding during their overnight stay there.

One week later Roger and Whitley took the Valentia to Risalpur to transport men and kit of B flight to fly to Bombay for defence scheme manoeuvres. They flew five hours from Risalpur to Jodhpur, then on the next day to Bombay with a break to refuel at Ahmadabad.

Bombay defence

Manoeuvres completed, several pints of beer consumed in the Mess, and they returned to Risalpur.

Manoeuvres

Once a year a strange game of 'Musical Squadrons' was played by the RAF. A Squadron from India would make the long flight to reinforce Singapore, usually for four weeks over Christmas. They would be replaced by a Squadron from Iraq, while one from England reinforced the Middle East, or 'Muddle East' as the RAF would jokingly call it.

In 1935 it was the turn of 39 Flight from Risalpur. The twelve Harts had been practising for weeks making short trips to land on emergency airstrips, the pilots carefully refuelling their own planes from the four gallon jerry cans stored there.

December 14th they set off with Roger and Whitley accompanying them in the Valentia carrying three crew, several airmen and spare parts including a whole Kestrel engine for the Harts. It was a journey of 4000 miles which they planned to make over six days with ten intermediate stops as the Harts had not got the 800 mile range of the Valentia. They flew to Ambala, and then on across the plains of the Punjab, on over the dry dusty flatness of central India to Cawnpore where the racecourse made a good makeshift landing ground.

The next destination was Calcutta some five hours away. The Harts stopped to refuel their planes at Gaya airstrip. When Roger spotted the huge muddy Hoogli delta he knew he was on course for Dum Dum,

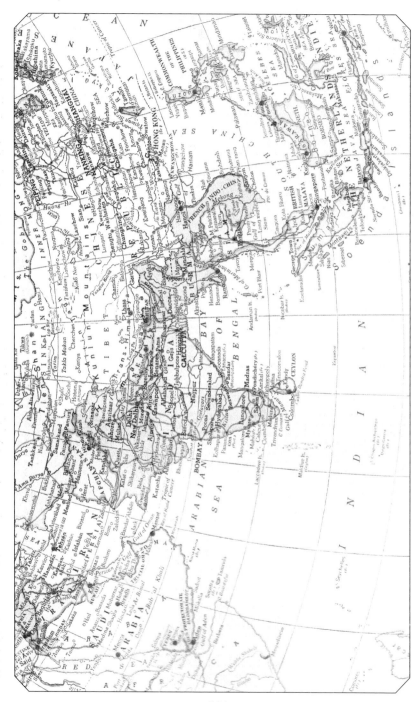

Lined up ready for take off

Calcutta's civil airport. Buses took them through the desperate poverty of the slums and they were welcomed to The Great Eastern Hotel by a sacred white Hindu cow lying on the steps. Inside the swing doors it was comfortable and cool, with the longest bar complete with brass foot rail, the furnishings a dark sort of Victorian time warp.

Next day they took off across the Hoogli Delta to cross the Bay of Bengal to Burma. Flying on a compass course, Roger and Whitley could see sparkling water through the broken cloud with occasional ships making for Calcutta. They crossed the coast at Chittagong with its low white red roofed buildings, the big plane swung right to follow the sandy palm fringed beaches to Akyab, landing on the single dusty airstrip perched on a plateau near the beach. The rich green vegetation was a welcome sight after the arid dust of northern India. Another three and a half hours flying over the jungle brought them to Rangoon the capital city of Burma. As they circled the golden dome of the Shwe Dagon, the Golden Pagoda, came into view, the gold leaf covering kept brilliant by the heavy rains.

After landing they were able to see this famous Buddhist temple, leaving their shoes outside. Inside the high gilded doors the huge jewel encrusted

Buddha dominated the space with an aura of deep calm. From the ground little could be seen of the golden dome, which seemed disappointing.

The Golden Pagoda

Next morning Roger woke to thick fog over Mingalad on Rangoon's rough sloping aerodrome. It soon cleared as the sun came up and they set off flying along the coastline of the Kra Isthmus which divides Burma from Siam

Four hours later a bright green square appeared in the tall rubber tree forest, Mergui. By lunchtime all the planes were safely down so there was time for some much needed maintenance and a chance to see the many spectators, and Burmese girls with gaily coloured parasols smoking and selling big cheroots, which they had reputedly rolled by hand on their thighs. A pleasant evening was spent in the Mergui Club, a tin hut with a good bar and some local Europeans including the uncrowned King of Burma who lived in a large untidy house near the aerodrome with five Burmese wives who all seemed very happy.

The Kra Isthmus

Next morning dawned fine, the heavy night rain over. The Valencia taxied off to the end of the runway, as it turned into wind one side dropped sharply, the wheels sunk in up to their axles. Luckily the wings and propellers were alright, and with much heaving on ropes and engine power the heavy aircraft was pulled free and able to take off for Alor Star in Malaya.

Roger found following the coastline not so easy because the mangrove swamps appeared to be land from the air but appeared as water on the map. The Harts stopped to refuel at a rough little airstrip near the coast, but Roger and Whitley flew on five and a half hours through rainstorms, the heat increasing to 80 degrees towards the Equator. Landing at Alor Star should be easy with a grass strip, and one tarmac one with drainage channels each side for the heavy rains, but a white cross on the grass strip signalled it was not to be used and a strong cross wind was blowing in gusts, not ideal after five hours of continuous flying, but they managed to land with more success than two of the Harts. With great ingenuity and burning the midnight oil the aircrew made one good plane from the two that slid off the runway. The plane with the crumpled wing, together with the pilot and the broken propeller were loaded onto the rail to Singapore in hopes that during their four weeks there it could be repaired.

Next morning Roger and Whitley took off at 8.35 for Seletar, the only RAF station on Singapore Island. The cumulus clouds piled up dark and thick and fast until a heavy monsoon rainstorm struck the Valentia, some of the rain poured off the wings backwards but visibility was very poor, so Roger swung out a bit to sea until the worst of the storm was over and bright sunshine showed the Straits of Johpur which separate the mainland from the Island of Singapore. Roger and Whitley stared ahead at a circular lake, unmarked on the map. A slow pass over the lake showed it to be surrounded by hangars and small planes, as they watched a small Hart made a splash landing creating quite a sizeable bow wave. The monsoon rains were slowly draining off the airfield and some grass was visible so they put the big plane down carefully to the relief of their three crew and four aircrew passengers. Quite a trip.

The Lake

Seletar boasted two Torpedo bomber squadrons and a Flying boat squadron as they flew mostly over the sea, a vivid contrast to the arid patrols of the Northwest Frontier.

Roger and Whitley were pleased to find they were staying in the Officers' Mess with the 39 squadron pilots. It was a modern building overlooking the Johore Strait with the Supermarine Flying boats bobbing at anchor.

Flying boats

The airmen stayed in a palm thatched barrack hut on the shore beside the Flying boat slipway and were allowed to bathe in the somewhat murky waters. The hangar for the Harts maintenance was only 200 yards away, and there was time between flying and maintenance to visit the city of Singapore.

Roger and Whitley had plenty of time to explore as they did not have the flying duties of 39 squadron who were experiencing the novelty and uncertainty of flying over water with bright reflections, and judging speed and distance of moving boats from various heights. Roger managed to 'borrow' a Hart for a short flight to see the harbour with the big white

P&O liners en route from London to Australia, some new war ships and the strangely shaped junks in a harbour which seemed like a city in itself.

There was much to see in Singapore where the European world meets the Eastern one. Sitting at the long bar in the Raffles Hotel, a gin sling in hand, cooled by the slowly revolving fans overhead the arid heat of India seemed a dream. When suitably refreshed the pilots would step out into the teeming multicultural world of Chinese, Polynesian and European people to choose a restaurant for the evening. Chinese dishes were so many and varied it was a popular choice.

Christmas at Seletar followed the pattern of RAF stations away from home, best decorated barracks, officers serving the airmen's Christmas dinner, parties, and some crazy sporting programme. This year it was a rugger game on the lawn of Government House, RAF versus the Navy from a ship anchored locally. The fumes of rum during the scrum were enough to overcome all but the strongest, and at half time the Navy did not provide lemons - just more rum – a barely remembered but most successful sporting fixture.

On into 1936 and the return to Risalpur. The crumpled Hart and its pilot had arrived by rail from Alor Star during the Christmas break and been repaired as best the riggers and fitters could do, even using some Osprey wings, courtesy of the Fleet Air Arm. It flew a little crabwise but with a twisted frame it was the best they could do. The pilot was delighted, so January 10th twelve Harts and Roger and Whitley in the Valentia set out on the return trip which went pretty smoothly. Finally crossing the Indus near Attock bridge, the familiar straight dusty road to Peshawar, and taxiing in to read a banner 'Well done 39 Welcome Home', and most of the men on the RAF station to welcome them in. A great start to 1936.

Roger's next assignment was to fly the Air Officer Commanding on a tour from Delhi to Karachi, so he and Whitley returned the Valentia to Lahore where they parted company. Plans were altered so Roger had time to write to his brother Dick, "At the moment I am in Delhi. The original idea was for one of our kites [planes] to go off on a State visit accompanying H E the Viceroy and Party to one of the native states down Bombay way. The other kite, ours, to collect the AOC (Air Officer Commanding) and his party and push off on a tour of inspection to Karachi. As things have turned out the Viceroy and party were recalled as soon as it was evident that the King was dying, and we have been detained here in Delhi. These Valentias of ours are doing sterling work. The Government won't push out any more budget to the RAF although it is palpably obvious that they are far in advance of the army from the viewpoint of utility and economy. Our two Valentias between them have flown close on 700 hours since they were delivered in August. We hear the King died last night so all the cinemas and restaurants have shut and most of the shops. We hear priceless rumours out here, the best one is that Prince Edward, or Edward VIII as he is now has abdicated, but no one knows who in favour of ! We fly to Singapore on 7th of next month and will be there 13 – 27 Feb this time with 60 Squadron in Wapitis what a life! You remember I signed on for 5 years, so I will be out of the Service when I return in June with 1500 flying hours to my credit. It's all very difficult to know what to do next. I could of course turn to civil flying, as I am fit and have the qualifications, I don't know, anyway I shall be back at the end of June if war is not declared. Cheerio Happy New Year   Roger".

Roger's time in Delhi was not wasted as he became a tourist to visit the famous Taj Mahal seeing the magnificent white building seeming to float on the water surrounding it. One of his photos, a close up of the onion dome could only have been obtained by 'borrowing' a small plane!

The Taj Mahal and 'Onion' Domes

The 'Onion' Domes

The AOC's tour did eventually take place, before Roger teamed up with Whitley to escort 60 Squadron from Kohat to Singapore. During his remaining time in India he practiced several hours of blind flying and qualified to fly on instruments.

There was a colossal leaving party with much Murree beer consumed. Some of the officers returning to their quarters were startled to see a motionless figure standing on his head in the gutter of a low roofed building. They had no doubt of Roger's ability to stand on his head as he did so regularly beside the bar with a pint on the floor beside him, but what if the gutter gave way....... to their relief he right sided himself, climbed down remarking "best part of the evening," and they made their way to bed.

The next day the Crossleys lined up to load men and baggage for the train at Peshawar and the bearers who accompanied them on the long journey to the quayside where the troop ship was waiting, new pale young pilots meeting their bearers, and collecting bistras, bronzed seasoned pilots and airmen boarding for uncertain futures in a changing world.

THE CALM BEFORE
——— THE STORM ———

The first thing Roger did after leaving the troopship at Southampton was to fly a Tiger Moth for half an hour, revelling in the freedom, the greenness below, and the cool air. Then the long train journey to Kirton where excited parents were waiting, followed by a splendid meal with his favourite Millers Pudding and a walk round the farm with his father.

Cousin Ian and Auntie Francie were the first to visit, swiftly followed by all the relations that lived near enough, eager to see Roger again and be regaled with tales of India.

Kirton Church seemed very quiet as the three Garvey girls were now married and Ronald away in a far corner of the Empire. The Thorntons had moved from Corringham Vicarage to Bournemouth as Janett's father had retired.

Roger soon bought his second car, a Hillman family saloon DEL 656 and set off to visit his sister Dulcie, taking some brightly coloured paper parasols for the four girls, his favourite nieces. What a splendid reunion, the girls were so excited they could hardly sit still for a photograph with Roger's new camera which had been such a success with the Indian photos.

Roger's next journey was to Bournemouth to see Janett where he got a warm welcome. Her father was not well so the young people went out a lot in the new car and it was not long before he proposed, Janett accepted, her father agreed and a splendid sapphire and diamond ring was bought. Janett's brother Maurice was home from South Africa with his wife

Jill, Ursula, Nic and Jo (sitting on a bench)

Kathleen and pretty little daughter Jill, so they rented a cottage and had a great time, the whole family together. Roger was intrigued to hear about the London theatres where Maurice was acting in a repertory company.

Jill and her Granny (Jill in pram)

Roger, Janett, Maurice and Kathleen

All too soon Roger was back to flying duties. His five years in the RAF had ended so he signed on again. Now he was 30 he could apply for Married Quarters, an officer's house, which he would move into with Janett after the wedding next year.

Roger found a room to rent near the airfield, and space for a workshop albeit a cellar. Some off duty time was spent in making a trailer to go behind the Hillman ready for the many moves he expected to make with Janett.

Janett's father, Reverend Robert Thornton

When the sturdy trailer was finished the day came to lift it out of the cellar. In spite of much effort from the officers mess and many beers he still had to take the wheels off to get it through the door.

The spring of 1937 was truly a time of moonlight and roses. When Roger was not flying or instructing he was with Janett. They traced the Thames to its source over many weeks of picnics and planning for their future.

The wedding plans were complete, Janett's cousins Disa and Mollie to be bridesmaids, her brother Maurice was acting in a repertory company in London so he would come down by train and don top hat and tails for the occasion. Roger's family made their plans to come, and Janett's beloved father would marry them.

Sadly his illness became worse and he died so the wedding was postponed, but Janett's mother insisted that it be not for long, so on July 7th 1937 the wedding took place in Bournemouth, with Maurice giving Janett away.

Janett with her brother Maurice

Janett with Roger

Arthur and Lucy, John and Anna, Dick

Janett's mother, Ethel, with her sisters Hally, Mab and Maudie

119

Roger and Janett settled into their new home making friends with the other officers and their wives.

Roger and Janett's new home

Roger went on a course of flying on instruments, which he would need to do at nights, and in an enclosed cockpit, so different to the big bi-planes with open cockpits he had flown in India.

Then followed a spell of Air Ministry work in an office with four other officers, very shut in. There was a telephone on a long cable. If it rang on Roger's desk and the call was not for him he would pick it up and walk over to the other desk with it. In no time a small hole appeared in the Air Ministry ceiling with a rod descending, ending in a long 'T' piece. One side had a counter balance, the other the phone. Now when it rang he only had to 'fly' it to the next desk amid cheers, and later on a few beers in the pub round the corner. May 6th 1938 a daughter was born and life was never the same again.

Jocelyn Crawfurd Maw

Roger's admin duties continued amid growing rumours of Hitler's changes in Europe. Janett settled down to life as an officer's wife, giving the required formal evening drinks parties for senior officers and their wives as their little daughter slept upstairs with the landing lights from the planes playing on the wall above her cot.

ON TARGET

September 1st 1939 Germany invaded Poland in a decisive and dreadful manner. The British Government honouring their Mutual Assistance Treaty of August 1939 had no option but to declare war on Germany on September 4th.

Great Britain came to a standstill as everyone gathered around the wireless in homes, offices, pubs and factories across the land. Everything stopped to hear the King's speech.

Wellington, the Geodetic Giant under construction

Strengthened by his strong message of working together for justice and liberty, Britain set about preparing for war. Shelters were built, sirens erected on street corners, hard hats were issued to the police. ARP

(Air Raid Precaution) wardens and first aiders were trained. Windows wore squares of white tape to save shattering in bomb blast, street lights switched off and blackout curtains made up at speed by the thousand yards. Sewing machinists were also in urgent demand for sewing miles of best Irish linen to cover the metal skeletons of Wellington bombers before they were covered in dope, and painted in their wartime colours.

Roger's elder brother John was recalled to the army, and his brother Dick joined the engineers.

Dick in the centre

The immediate effect of the war on Arthur and Lucy at Cleatham was the silence of the empty house – one last photograph – a roar of exhaust smoke and they were all gone.

Janett's brother Maurice joined the Royal Fusiliers in the City of London Regiment.

January 1940 Roger was sent on a course on poison gas to Porton's Lark Hill, not the best of experiences. Next was a Maintenance Liaison course, so secret he said he hadn't the faintest idea what he maintained

Lucy with two of her boys, Roger and Dick, in uniform

Roger's brother, John

or who he liaised with! To his surprise his next mission was to go to France to drive a lorry of poison gas home to England, so it could not be used in anger or propaganda by the advancing Germans. Driving in a convoy those long tree-lined roads seemed endless. There was always a big tailback at each of the main crossroads, the British army directing traffic. As he neared the head of one queue Roger noticed something familiar about the army officer on the crossroads. He stopped the engine and leapt out "John old boy", "Roger". John halted all six lanes of traffic as they had a brief reunion, neither

Maurice in his new uniform

knowing that within days the horror of Dunkerque would engulf so many.

During Roger's brief leave he and Janett decided that she and baby Jocelyn would be safer in Bournemouth with her mother, rather than living on an aerodrome. So they loaded the trailer and set off.

Roger and Jocelyn with Mrs Thornton

Mrs Thornton was delighted, and welcomed them with open arms, she and her sister were already knitting balaclavas and socks for the troops. Roger made a wooden frame for the big landing window and covered it with chicken wire, and helped to run tapes across the other windows to prevent flying glass. He also helped to bolt the big metal Morrison shelter together in the dining room which they would climb into in case of air raids, knowing they would be safe even if the house was bombed.

Roger's next posting was to Bassingbourn to learn to fly a Wellington bomber. Designed by Barnes Wallis who had also worked on airship design including the R100.

The Wellington known to most aircrew as the Wimpey was made of a geodetic lattice work of metal strips, covered by fabric and painted with 'dope' to strengthen and waterproof it. The twin-engine bomber measured 65 feet long with an 80 foot wing span. It carried a crew of six, the captain or first pilot, second pilot, wireless operator, navigator who was also the bomb aimer, and front and tail gunners.

Roger and his fellow pilots were issued with a handbook of Pilot's notes, just over forty pages which took some digesting.

The Wellington Bomber

Pilot's instrument panel

127

All aircrew had to learn the emergency exits, crash drill, fire drills and how to pump the oil round the engines on long flights.

Wellington bombers were being produced by the hundred and a propaganda film was made of workers in the Vickers factory assembling a complete Wellington in 24 hr 48 min. They carried in, assembled, and welded the metal sections together, installed the pipework and electrics. The pilot's seat, cockpit floor and control column came in one piece. The heavier items self sealing bullet proof fuel tanks, rear turret and engines were carried into position by cranes moving on gantries in the roof, all driven by women. The skeleton was covered by Irish linen, eight stitches to the inch, and bolted to the frame, some final stitches, all inspected and covered by nine coats of dope.

As so many Wellington bombers were being produced many new pilots were needed, so Roger met men from all over Britain and beyond as they struggled to master the complexities of the Wimpey.

During the initial training Janett was able to visit Roger with their little daughter who vividly remembers her father going up a huge ladder with lots of men into a plane (the ladder had six rungs!).

Roger and little Joshey

Climbing in

Roger was soon on ops over France, 'Nickel' dropping. They dropped propaganda leaflets to encourage the German people to surrender. This gave the pilots and crew experience of the plane without the weight of bombs.

July 27th 1940 Squadron Leader Maw and five crew took off at 21.50 for several sites in France 'Nickel' dropping. Mission completed they headed home in bright moonlight, with some low cloud.

Within thirty miles of Bassingbourn the starboard engine spluttered and died. As the big plane lost height, all Roger's early training came to the fore as he searched for a suitable field to land in. The fields were small with big hedges – he instructed the crew to lie on the floor and brace themselves for landing against the main spar "then get out and run like hell towards the road". There was a crashing of branches as they tore through a hedge, then silence. By the roadside they found Roger wasn't with them. Sergeant Patterson ran back to find Roger still in the pilot's seat – "got my leg wrapped round the stick!". It was a double fracture and took months to mend. It was as the crew said later, "a brilliant landing – just in the wrong place!"

During the ensuing months in hospital with pins and weights and pulleys on his leg, Roger's son Michael was born.

He couldn't wait to get home and take photos.

As convalescence progressed Joshey's dolls house took shape, and to the ward sister's dismay tiny shavings of wood and scraps of material to cover the tiny armchairs fell from his bed on to the spotless ward floor.

Ronald Garvey wrote a letter from the Pacific.

Four months later Roger was 'flying solo' without crutches.

Michael Robert Seaton Maw makes his entrance, with Nurse and Joshey

Janett, her mother with Joshey and Mike

UNIQUE

I CLAIM TO BE THE ONLY FULLY CURED PATIENT

AT LEAST
THATS WHAT I THINK

PROOF
I NO LONGER NEED
(1) TEA AT ALL TIMES OF THE DAY or NIGHT
(2) BREAKFAST IN BED
(3) STICKS
(4) REMEDIAL EXERCISES
(5) LEAVE
(6) SYMPATHY OR THE, DOC

Proof!

The photos of his new son came out well and it was good to have time together before his next posting to his beloved Lincolnshire to Binbrook, high on the Wolds.

130

British Residency
Vila, New Hebrides
29th December 1940

Dear Roger

By the last budget of news from Kirton I gleaned the information from Trixie, my best correspondent, that you were hobbling about on crutches as a result of giving Adolf a kick in the behind, or some such excellent exploit. You have no idea how much I admire and envy you. If only I could get a crack at that gentleman's posterior, what a packet of epsom salts I would deliver.

Since the war began I expect that you have been far too busy to attend to letter writing, as I have. If war your side of the world means bombs, our side here it means bumph.... acres of it. The telegraphic correspondence has increased by leaps and bounds, and that means aeons of time spent in cyphering and coding. We do our best to help in these odd parts of the world, but it is very depressing not to be in the thick of it. I tried to get to England, but was pipped on the post as I was recalled to duty here. The Colonial Service is one of these ruddy reserved occupations classes so that there is not the faintest chance of being released for Home Service.

It makes me very wild when I think of all the energy I have wasted from 1935 onwards writing Memoranda about the defence of the Pacific by air, and the whole ruddy place is overrun by raiders which my projected Bases could have mopped up before breakfast. As I expect you know a raider shelled Nauru the other day; one of my bases was only 400 miles away, and Oh what a shock that raider could have got.

Pat has just reminded me that I must congratulate on the arrival of a son and heir in August last. Well done Janet. Anthony, your godson, is now on the way to six and is a remarkable handful. Thank heaven he has started to go to school, which mops up a certain amount of his energy, as he shakes the average small tropical house to its foundations.

Love from all to all
Yours aye
RH Garvey
PS I don't know your rank so am demoting you on the envelope to 'Esq'.

12 Squadron was newly equipped with Wellingtons, so Roger's role as flight commander was to include a lot of training at nights, and on fine clear days formation flying, bombing and gunnery practice, cross country, and air to sea targets over the same area as he had flown from Waddington in training.

There was much training of new crew, and pilots on dual instruction until the crews were operationally fit. On foggy days there were lectures on first aid and use of oxygen, and the techniques of navigation and bomb aiming.

By April 1941 the squadron was carrying out their first all Wellington bombing raids into France. April 9th Wing Commander Blackden's plane was missing over the North Sea, a great loss to the squadron as two of his crew were bombing and gunnery leaders.

Wellington 5361. Roger flew this over Cologne

The next morning Squadron Leader Maw was called into the office and Wing Commander Roger Maw stepped out to assume command of 12 Squadron. With the increased responsibility and paperwork Roger was glad he had found a room on a hill top farm locally with the Robinsons. It was good to be lulled into sleep by a tractor and cows after a night raid.

There were enemy planes overhead at times and all station activity halted by Red Alert on the siren. One day Roger was reaching into his locker for his flying kit – the next moment he was stepping out of his locker into a sea of broken glass, not a window left intact. Regular bombing raids were launched from Binbrook and as commanding officer, Roger did not fly every time but saw them take off at 10.30 p.m. and waited to count them in and take the reports at 4 or 5 a.m. When he did fly as first pilot and captain it was often with a different crew each time so he got to know his men, five at a time, second pilot, navigator, wireless operator and two gunners.

Part of Roger's work was to organize leave passes for each man at Binbrook, ensuring enough aircrew and ground staff at all times. Rex Wheeldon's wedding had a high priority. August 11th 1941 was a fine day and confetti was scattered from a lone Wimpey!

Rex Wheeldon's wedding, Roger second from the left

Roger's leave often took him over the Wolds to Cleatham for time with his parents and brother Dick, a keen member of the Territorials and an expert electrical engineer. His work with a searchlight battery to the north east of the county gave him some time at home to help Arthur with the farm. He regaled them with tales of a local farmer's wife supplying the ack ack and searchlight crews with her mangold wurzel wine – one glass was very warming but after three you couldn't see the searchlight!

Atlantic convoys were suffering heavy losses and three of Germany's most destructive battleships the Gneisenau, Scharnhorst and Prinz Eugen were regularly serviced and repaired across the Channel.

A big daylight raid was planned for July. There were to be two levels of bombers, three at 3000 feet to draw the flak with Roger flying the leading plane, and the rest of the squadron at 12,000 feet to drop the heavy armour piercing bombs. Roger chose his crew and instructed them to write letters home and give them to non flying crew. At the briefing the seven crews settled on the benches, the door shut and the curtain swept aside from the map of the target - the battleship Gneisenau.

The Scharnhorst

It was to be a daylight raid to the docks in Brest – one of the most heavily defended areas. Roger's plane carried an extra man, a fire control officer, his wireless operator Richard Copey had little space so he stood behind the second pilot, Sergeant McKnight, with a good view forward. There was terrific noise as the ack ack guns below opened up, the two wing men dived away from the searchlights and Roger was thrown off course so they had to go round again – the smell of cordite was strong and Richard heard Roger mutter "this is a dicey do" as they flew into the heaviest flak. Richard noticed the altimeter plunge from 4000 feet to 2000, the plane gathering speed as the bombs hit, and he saw a ME109 dive away, hearing a comment "109 destroyed" from the rear gunner Sergeant Lewis. The navigator shouted bombs gone and Roger dived away to wave top height and headed for home, 100 feet above them Sergeant Elsdon was wrestling with the controls of his damaged Wimpey. They made it back to Binbrook flak damaged and exhausted after almost 7 hours flying. Only Sergeant

Heald and his crew failed to return. A letter was subsequently written to King George VI outlining the daylight raid on the German battleships at Brest where bombers encountered extremely heavy and accurate anti-aircraft fire, fighter opposition and a balloon barrage.

Success due to bravery, determination and resource shown by the pilots and aircrew resulted in Roger being invited to the Palace to be awarded the DFC (Distinguished Flying Cross), with his rear gunner for his award.

Daylight bombing was so costly that from now on Binbrook Wimpeys were ordered on night raids.

Bombing up a Wellington

There were rumours of Hitler's invasion, and from the number of German planes it was obvious there was to be no let up by the RAF who were regularly flying off at 11 p.m. and returning from their targets at dawn. One aircraft had the landing gear shot away but did a belly landing successfully reminding Roger forcefully with memories of Clophill, so he made sure that every crew knew the many escape routes from the Wimpey not just up the ladder beneath the tail The designer, Barnes Wallis, had thoughtfully provided a starboard push out panel, a roof exit in the pilot's cockpit with two outwardly opening doors operating from a central lever, and the sextant dome above the wings. One or two planes brought their three 500 lb bombs home as they couldn't find the target which provided some heart stopping moments.

Officers' Mess, 12 and 147 Squadron aircrew, Binbrook, Summer 1941. Roger tenth from left front row.

On September 7th 1941 19 aircraft took off from Binbrook with planes from neighbouring aerodromes for Berlin to bomb a large railway station. It was cloudy as the Wellingtons droned over the coast and on across sleeping Germany, taking an indirect course to avoid the fighters. Then the sky cleared as they approached Berlin, it was brilliantly lit with what seemed to be hundreds of searchlights and a solid wall of flak – the noise was deafening and the smell of cordite strong. Six aircraft were hit and Roger's rear gunner's parachute harness, tunic and shirt were torn by a shell splinter, luckily he wasn't injured. There is a legend that Roger looped the loop, or did a victory roll on this occasion "to show the bastards they can't bomb London and get away with it". If so what happened to the Elsan toilet in the tail section one doesn't like to think! Two aircraft failed to return so there were more letters for Roger to write.

As the numbers of Wellingtons dwindled they were replaced, flown up from the Vickers Aircraft Factory by the ATA (Air Transport Auxiliary) or 'Ancient and Tired Airmen' as the aircrew called them, but to Roger and the ground crews amazement the diminutive blonde who stepped from the neatly landed Wellington was neither ancient nor tired. "I've got time for a beer before my taxi comes" was her opening statement. Roger discovered over the beer in the mess that Maureen was part of a growing band of female delivery pilots, and her 'taxi' was a small plane piloted by another one. She had flown all sorts, fighters and bombers.

On September 15th 1941 Roger handed over the command of 12 Squadron to Wing Commander BJR Roberts and set off for a brief leave at Cleatham before going to Bournemouth for a time with Janett and the children. He couldn't believe how much the children had grown, Mikey now just over a year and Joshey $2\frac{1}{2}$.

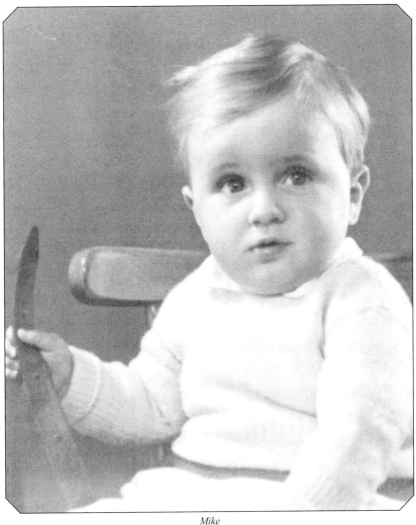

Mike

Roger's next posting was to Kinloss in Scotland as chief flying instructor. As it overlooked the Moray Firth and there was a 50% chance of landing in water his first question to the new pilots was "how well do you swim"!

Wapitis, Wellingtons and Binderband

The RAF referred to Kinloss as Dead Loss, too far from Inverness for a night out it seemed remote from war or home. Boredom was alleviated by the laird and his wife who held regular dinner parties for the young officers.

In March 1942 Roger had a brief leave with Janett, her mother, and the children during which he serviced the car and buried a 5 gallon drum of petrol for her to use in case of invasion. Precious photos were taken and he left for Harwell to take a Wellington to the Middle East.

Janett, Joshey and Mike

Joshey and Mike

—THE MUDDLE EAST—

Harwell was a busy place. The engineers were fitting extra fuel tanks to the Wellingtons in their bomb bays, navigators had detailed instructions of the long route and its potential dangers. Tropical kit was issued – long shorts, thick Khaki shirts and a pith helmet which reminded Roger of India. Roger's crew came together and started filling every space on the Wimpey with a minimum of personal belongings and as many stores as they could manage for Malta.

At 4 a.m. the overloaded plane struggled off the runway and the crew settled to their tasks, resting when they could. The dawn came up bright, and extra care was taken searching the skies for German fighters. Over the Bay of Biscay and skirting the coast of Spain, which was neutral and no military flights were allowed over there. The brilliant white beaches of Portugal slid beneath them. Ten and a half hours later the tiny Rock of Gibraltar appeared almost surrounded by blue green sea. They saw a short sandy landing strip on the old race course, the fuel gauge on empty Roger swung in over the sea and braked hard. They stepped out into red hot sunshine.

Next morning after a sociable evening the crew climbed into the Wimpey for a tricky take off.

No-one slept on this leg of the journey with German guns and fighters on Sicily, Italians listening on the radio, and convoys of shipping below which could open up gunfire at any time.

After eight hours the front gunner spotted Malta, it seemed so tiny, alone, vulnerable. The Grand Harbour at Valletta came into view, and Roger

A Wellington taking off from Gibraltar with an anti-submarine patrol in the foreground

set the Wimpey down gently with a sigh of relief on Luqa airfield, the only one with a proper runway. As they landed an air-raid siren wailed and everyone disappeared underground where most people seemed to be living – emerging to swim in the sea between raids.

Two uneasy days later they took off again, lighter from the stores but with a passenger, an 'air comode' with luggage. The wireless operator showed him how to pump oil to the engines when needed on the long journey. Roger flew low when the navigator warned him of dangers and all was well until a brilliant flash of lightning. Roger automatically threw the plane, weaving about the sky thinking it was searchlights. The 'air comode' was thrown into the depths of the tail shouting "What the hell!". Roger grinning answered "Just a spot of turbulence sir!".

At last the Nile delta came into view, brilliant green against the barren rocky surroundings. No soft sand, not a palm tree in sight. Roger eased the Wimpey down to the Middle East Pool on the Sweet Water Canal, they emerged to its stinking smell, raging heat, choking dust and all those flies. Accommodation was in bell tents, and the only facilities the mess tent and the NAAFI tent where they got to know fellow fliers over a few lukewarm beers. It seemed to Roger that each squadron was a mobile unit, flexible to move at the drop of a hat to advanced landing grounds, nearer the targets, flying up during the heat of the day to refuel and take on bombs in the cool of the evening before night flying on operations. The engineers, spares and stores would make its perilous way overland in long sweating convoys.

Desert convoy

The landing grounds had improvised runways scraped from the desert. Numbers of planes on a raid varied each night depending on available spares to patch up damage from last night's raid, and who had 'Gippy tummy'. Lines of warfare flowed back and forth as Monty's 8th Army fought back Rommel's Afrika Corps from the canal zone.

Bombing policy came from the War Cabinet and was translated into targets on a bombing form with number of aircraft required, bomb type and load etc.

May 1st 1942 Roger assumed command of 108 Squadron at Fayid.

Squadron badge

The squadron consisted of a cheerful mixture of Wellingtons and American Liberators with their crews and mechanics. The Liberators had four engines and a crew of ten. The first night they took off with their bombs at dusk for a code named raid and returned almost 14 hours later. Roger's eight Wellingtons took off to wreak havoc on Benghazi, the Afrika Corps main supply port, and the oil tanks by Portalago Bay. All returning safely at dawn.

Almost every night some planes went off, one night a Liberator was missing so Roger assumed temporary command of them as well. Engine trouble, dawn mist, haze over the targets, and sandstorms were regular hazards.

Wellington wrapped against sandstorms

As the Wellingtons were flying such long hours to reach their targets it was decided to send more to the advanced landing ground where they could do some maintenance but to keep most of the spares, cannibalized aircraft, and engineers to do larger repairs, back at Fayid for 37, 70 and 108 squadrons.

May 22nd 1942 it was Roger's turn to go on ops – briefing at 12 o'clock revealed the target for the eight Wellingtons - the port of Benghazi.

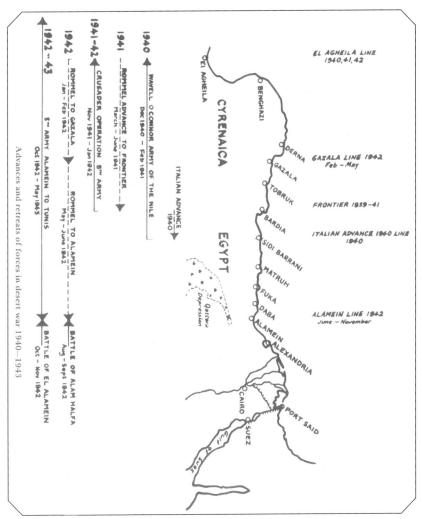

Map of the Muddle East

The Wimpeys were towed to the end of the runway (to prevent the Merlin engines overheating). The two pilots took their seats, the rest of the crew on two suspended beds – normal for take off and landing. The plane was like an oven, no-one wearing much more than flying boots, shorts and helmet, being careful not to burn themselves on exposed metal. The engines roared, they bumped over uneven ground and as they climbed the temperature dropped, open windows and hatches provided a cool breeze on the way to Landing Ground 105.

143

After landing there was the usual mad rush to the beer tent, then a walk to the Mess tent for a meal, followed by a few hours sleep in the plane. Roger woke them in time to change into flying clothes and Mae Wests, last cigarettes extinguished and they were off again. Roger's plane carried flares to light the target for the following Wimpeys. They lit the target up like day. Blinding searchlights combing the sky, guns below roaring, each plane bombing his allotted target – some having to go round a second time, Roger saw several fires below. The moment the word came 'Bombs away' he weaved through the remaining searchlights and flak and headed for the landing ground. That night they all came home safely.

The beer tent

Roger noted in his summary for May that only one plane went missing - Liberator AL511 but he felt there was a good chance of the crew being prisoners of war. He recorded the squadron's pride at the awards of Bar to DFC Flying Officer Anderson, Distinguished Flying Cross to Squadron Leader D R Bagnall and Distinguished Flying Medals to Sergeant M Collenette and Flight Sergeant G S W Challen.

During May 1942 108 Squadron had flown 539 operational hours in 73 sorties, dropping over 73 tons of bombs. Roger recorded "Once again the

Squadron is maintaining a very high standard of operational efficiency and the results reflect the greatest credit on the ground staff".

In June they were flying from Landing Ground 105 against Benghazi, Derna on the coast west of Tobruk, Timimi satellite aerodrome and Martuba landing ground to discourage the German Luftwaffe. During this time their landing ground was attacked by a German raider dropping butterfly bombs. Two armourers were killed. They were buried at El Daba in the cemetery. Roger wrote their letters home to next of kin and recorded it in his report, also "The Squadron lost two Wellingtons this month", Roger recorded "and their loss was keenly felt".

The Liberators moved on which was a blow to the ground staff as their engineers were such good experienced men and always keen to help out with the Wellingtons.

Towards the end of June enemy tanks were advancing across the desert and in one night twenty two sorties were carried out by Roger's 108 Wellingtons, some going up a second time bombing ammunition trucks, petrol bowsers, tanks and convoys. Then coming down to as low as fifty feet to destroy the enemy's war machine. Some crews reported machine gun fire tearing through the fabric of their aircraft but no casualties reported and all made it back safely to base.

Orders were received to move to RAF station Kabrit under the HQ No. 236 Wing. Everything was packed up in one day, the convoy leaving at dawn and taking two days to travel via Cairo but the planes carried the essential ground crew in one flight so operations could continue to attack the enemy army concentrations that night. As they approached Kabrit Roger saw a tarmac runway, permanent sand coloured buildings and hangars, with the Great Bitter Lake nearby.

After landing they were allocated sleeping quarters, tents near the lake. They soon learned that both RAF and army were pulling back from the desert to the canal zone.

Every night Roger's squadron sent up as many as ten Wellingtons to attack the enemy army in the desert which attracted the Luftwaffe with JU88s attacking. Most of the Wimpeys returned to Kabrit, one did a belly landing in the desert but the crew were alright. Daily repairs were needed and the worst hit aircraft broken up for spares. In his summary of June 1942 Roger noted "Great credit must be given to the older flying crews of the squadron, who, although having already completed one tour of operations responded to the call. It is felt that the efforts shown during the last few days have had a tremendous effect on the morale and striking forces of the enemy."

Early one morning a coded signal was received. Roger as commanding officer was to fly with his crew and two other Wellingtons, no bombs, their destination a secret until take off. Once in the air the navigator opened the sealed orders and guided Roger to a desert landing ground - he noticed a lot of army transport and a couple of small planes parked up. Landing neatly at 9 a.m. they were met by an army officer and a smell of bacon. "Report to the mess tent" was all he would say. Inside long trestle tables, hundreds of army and some RAF personnel. There was a top table at the far end and there in a haze of cigar smoke sat a familiar figure. Beside him was General Montgomery. After a hearty breakfast Winston Churchill gave a speech Roger and his crews would never forget, and they were thanked by General Montgomery for their assistance.

July 1942 Kabrit. One of the other squadrons Wellingtons crashed in flames on take off but the rear gunner was recovered unharmed, still in his turret in 4 feet of water in the lake!

Early July large numbers of Roger's Wellingtons took off every night to attack enemy convoys and camps in the Daba area returning safely despite heavy anti-aircraft fire, Roger taking his turn. The navy's Albacores dropping flares to illuminate the area were a great help.

On July 5th Wellington L was attacked by a JU88 firing canon, the rear gunner replied and the captain took violent evasive action down to seventy feet where he managed to climb out of the dive in spite of the controls being jammed. The Captain, Flight Sergeant Metcalf, managed to land the badly damaged aircraft but the wireless operator had died.

July 7th against all odds, Sergeant Ackerman turned up, wireless operator of aircraft A lost over the Sidi Barrani area nine days earlier. He reported the Wellington attacked by a JU88 and caught fire, all except the rear gunner parachuted out and landed safely. He fell in with a forward unit of 7th Armoured Division, and a field ambulance found his front gunner Sergeant J Brookes, so Roger was able to write a second more hopeful letters to the relatives of that crew.

After two weeks of continuous operations the squadron had a 'stand off' day which was appreciated by all. The target was now Tobruk and its busy harbour, which was so well defended.

Roger was writing reports when there was a hell of an explosion, he rushed out to see a mass of flames, the   bb fire truck could do nothing, nor the ambulance.

Armourers hoisting 250 lb bombs into a Wellington

Aircraft S was being 'bombed up', a 40 lb bomb was accidentally dropped and just exploded in the heat. When the fires died down Roger went out alone to gather what he could of the five brave men who died and returned to write to their families. That night twelve Wellingtons set out across the scarred runway to attack enemy units in the Daba area. Then they resumed ops on Tobruk, its harbour and shipping by now Rommel's main supply line.

Roger's July report

Operational hours flown	No. of sorties	Tonnage of bombs
2082.25	314	310

Roger noted the squadron's effort this month had been outstanding with special praise to the Ground crew.

August 1st 1942 Roger recorded "Today marks the first anniversary of the Squadron. Over one year of extensive operations against the enemy only twelve aircraft failed to return. This reflects the greatest credit on both aircrew and ground crews indicating that the Squadron has been fortunate in having personnel of such high standard of skill and efficiency."

During the first three weeks of August they bombed Tobruk and its heavily defended harbour almost every night. Both men and machines were very tired. Caffeine tablets to counteract lack of sleep, quick repairs and more oil for the aircraft. Every night that he was not flying Roger would see his planes leave, watching the air from the propellers ruffle the Great Bitter Lake as they rumbled off into the moonlit sky at around 8 p.m., sometimes they would return early with engine trouble, occasionally a heart stopping landing with bombs still on board. Any length of sleep was not possible as he was always there when they came into land, taking the de-briefing, piecing what information he could of any missing aircraft, and how successful the raid had been. August was a bad month, four planes went missing, but one flew back to base entirely on one engine, another landed in the Qattara Depression area and the crew were rescued by friendly tanks. The squadron moved to another landing ground on the Cairo Alexandria road continuing to fly every night.

Over the years as a bomber pilot Roger had devised many original ideas on operational tactics, beginning with his experience over the German warship Gneisenau when he went over at 4000 feet and dropped to 2000 feet to pick up speed which also confused the gunners who set their sights to fire at one height. The Maw plan was adopted over Tobruk, aircraft arriving early circled outside the flak zone then at an agreed time they all went over the target on a given heading together. This limited period of intense bombing swamped the defences and helped to lessen the casualties, provided the home base could be easily reached without running out of fuel. Roger had spent so many anxious hours watching planes coming home after a raid, landing within minutes of each other on the same runway unable to go round again - some barely taxiing before the fuel ran out. He always made sure there were enough ground crew with vehicles ready to tow one out of the way if necessary.

August 27th Roger again took off for Tobruk but had to turn back owing to starboard generator trouble, this put right he took off again and decided to attack the battle area destroying fuel and arms stores.

Another night there was a double sortie on the battle area - the first sortie of seven Wellingtons took off at 8.30 p.m., returned just before midnight, and hour and a half later, bombed up and refuelled, they took off again, all returned safely. The squadron's diary recorded "This double sortie was largely instrumental in preventing a successful enemy attack."

During August they flew 1164.55 operational hours, 251 sorties, and dropped 327 tons of bombs.

September began with a hope for new crews as so many had completed their tour of duty, 30 ops. The target now was mainly the battle area with little opposition, then back to Tobruk where they used the Maw plan with some success.

September 19th 1942, six Wimpeys were detailed to attack Tobruk, one failed to return. W sent out an SOS but Roger's attempt to give their position in plain language was lost in radio interference. The squadron's diary records great regret that Wing Commander R H Maw DFC, Sergeant N R Millson (Second Pilot), Sergeant F Greenstein (Navigator), Sergeant G Bennett (Wireless Operator), Sergeant R L Berry (Front Gunner) and Sergeant B E Doublard (Rear Gunner) failed to return. Wing Commander C Gibson DFC took over command of 108 Squadron and records "Wing Commander R H Maw DFC by his cheerful disposition and enthusiasm for operations, made himself very popular with all ranks. He had many original ideas for operational tactics and some were adopted by higher authorities. At all times he tried to improve the conditions of the airmen, and his efforts in that direction were greatly appreciated."

What happened next is recorded in Roger's diary (extract follows).

20th September 1942

At about 00.35 the starboard engine suddenly splutterd and ceased to function. We jettisoned all we could, but, lost height rapidly. After a while it became obvious we could not make it and as the country below appeared very broken and a mass of wadis – I ordered the Crew to abandon.

A few minutes later after signaling 3 times on the emergency light to make sure the tail gunner had gone (I had seen the others go), I abandoned myself. I reduced speed to 100 m.p.h. and leaving the engine full on I quickly left the control and dropped out facing the tail, hand on the ring. The height indicated was 1000 feet the ground was 600 feet (ie about 6 to 800 feet above ground level only, taking into account the altimeter setting).

When the parachute opened the pack hit me sharply under the chin and knocked me half silly! However, I quickly realised I was swivelling round rapidly like a joint on the spit. I shook the rigging lines, but the moment the paracute was under control, I hit the ground - just a few seconds before I was ready for it and twisted my left leg badly, rendering my ankle extremely painful and also my knee to some extent. The right leg was fortunately perfectly O.K.

I lay for a moment or two wondering a hundred things - was my leg broken? How far had I to go? What had happened to the others? Had they all got out and were they all right? No one had any water! Of course it was over in a few seconds - this period of recovery, when I heard a distant thud and almost at once the old familiar flames spurted up, together with the all too often seen pall of black smoke, but, as I sat there I thought - "It is not half as much as I should have expected!"

I decided I must get to the wreckage as that would be my only hope of meeting up with any of my Crew, all of whom where raw, new to the desert and probably hardly knew North from South by the stars, let alone the sun.

It was a painful job in the half moon light, stumbling among rocks and over the most incredibly uneven ground, and after an hour I lay down to rest still quarter of a mile away from the burning wreckage: the hike had to be made before the fire went out, just in case I missed it and had misjudged the distance, so I went on taking bearings by the moon as I descended into a deep, dry wadi out of sight of the spluttering fire that was all that seemed to be left of the old kite.

That last bit down into the wadi and up the other side was just Hell, but, at last I topped the rise and came on the burnt out Wimpey sooner than I expected. It had taken me three hours and I felt pretty done in, so I lay down by the port wing which curiously enough was almost intact, and dozed until dawn. I could not sleep: it was too bitterly cold and very damp. I just relaxed and waited until it was light enough to take stock of the situation.

It is queer how the sense of self preservation asserts itself at times of stress. I lay and figured out quite impartially that if I could only find a suitable piece of wreckage to use as a stick, I would make perhaps $1^1/_2$ m.p.h., and if it was 30 miles to the coast road, that meant 20 hours walking. I'd have to rest 3 hours in the heat of the day and it looked as if my ankle was too bad to travel at all by night unless the going got much smoother: that meant 2 and possibly up to 3 days without water or food. For a while I was greatly perturbed as I could not verify the North Star - I was pretty sure I knew which one it was, but, I could not figure out the 'Plough'. At last I pieced things together: some of the stars of the Plough were very indistinct as they were so low and because of the moon which, although not full was giving quite a lot of light. I took careful note of the North Star bearing mentally, and checked this by the rising sun when the time came.

As soon as it was light I looked over the wreckage and found first of all a dural tube 5 feet long: just the thing for helping me along on the duff leg. A futher discovery was the dinghy almost complete, though somewhat the worse for wear and of all the incredible luck a water bottle nearly full of fresh water - plus a number of rations. Further back among the wreckage were numerous items which had been in the cabin on the bed before the crash.

My chute bag was there torn partly open and my pistol with belt and 30 rounds all intact; even the 'safe passage' chit was there out in the early morning dew, and my silk map of Lybia. I also found a first aid kit and a useful knife all part of the dinghy equipment.

By 8.30 I was ready for the long trek, with a pack comprising my battle dress top, half a flare parachute and some strips of rubberised material cut out of the Dinghy; also the marine distress signals - just in case! The water bottle and 2 boxes of rations together with the first aid outfit and revolver completed the pack.

The question of my crew afforded me not a little worry but at this juncture I reasoned that the kite had burned brightly for at least 3 hours and spasmodically for a further three right up to dawn breaking and still no one had come over: add to which it was 7½ hours after the crash before I set out, so I reasoned the other lads must have set off for the Coast at once, and were most unlikely to be attempting to locate the wreckage. It was their lack of water and rations that caused me most anxiety, not to mention the awful consequences a broken limb might have: Further to this I wondered very much whether they would be able to steer at all acurately if any of them got separated from the others.

However, I was in no form myself to search for them, and I knew I should need all my strength, especially if my leg got any worse: so I limped away from the wreckage, heading as near 10° West of North as I could guess and judge my time and sun.

That day and the next were hell. I took two fair mouthfulls of water and sucked 3 Horlicks tablets for breakfast and then kept up 50 minutes march, or rather hobble and 10 minutes rest. I rested 2 hours from 11.30 to 1.30 and a futher 45 minutes at the next stop as the heat was awful between 1.30 and 2.15 and I knew I could not afford to lose more sweat than could be helped.

I last looked back at the old kite at 10.00 just before leaving the last brow of a hill from which I could see it, and still none of the others had found it.

The going was rough and I kept twisting my duff ankle, but, it seemed I was covering the best part of two miles per march which encouraged me no end. The crash was some five miles to the south of the edge of a line of clearly defined hills which at this point lie some 30 miles inland from the coast by Sidi Barami, and before leaving the top of these hills, I looked out towards the North and to the sea and my goal - the Coast Road.

The distance seemed enormous. I could not see the sea although the morning was clear and remarkably free of haze. It was best not to think of the distances involved, but, rather to concentrate on getting the most out of my 1½ pints of water and the Horlicks tablets.

I had a good 3 or 4 square yards of parachute made in the form of a turban on my head for sun protection and in the mid day rests I slung my turban and the other parachute silk over the dural tube and a handy thorn bush to make plenty of shade. I took off my boots and stockings and really relaxed. This is absolutely essential in the desert especially when you aren't used to it.

At 7.30 I decided to pack in. It had been a long day: in fact apart from 3 or 4 hours lying down, you could not call it sleeping, the previous night I had not slept a wink for 36 hours. I took off my boots and sat down under the lee side of a large green bush and consumed 3 Horlicks tablets and a little chocolate concentrate, not to mention two mouthfuls of water. The water was lasting well, being only one third consumed when I lay down to sleep. The ground was hard, but, I slept well with my bits of parachute over me and the top coverings of bits cut from the dinghy to keep the dew off.

21st September 1942

I was awake with the first light and stiff, but, feeling remarkably refreshed. My ankle was still very swollen and bruises were begining to show up, but, when it was firmly bound and assisted to some extent with the splint of bits of wood, I had devised, it seemed no worse than the day before and indeed after ½ an hour it seemed a lot better.

My watch ceased to function during the first march and refused to go for any length of time from then on. This was rather a blow to my 'Boy

Scout' method of telling the direction by the sun so I had to guess it all that day.

At that time of year however in North Africa there is almost invariably a sea breeze blowing by day and it is North and tends to have some West in it. This wind is effective for some way inland and I used this as a check on my guess by the sun.

I knew I must conserve my strength in case I had misjudged distances and in order to cater for a 3rd days march if need be: consequently as my leg was going a lot better and it was damn nearly (if not quite) a full moon that night, I decided to lay up for four hours through the heat of the day and carry on two marches after dark.

From time to time it seemed I could see the sea in the distance but it is most dangerous to build up hope of this sort in the desert: You have to force your imagination into the background, make a plan and stick rigidly to it, and believe nothing you **think** you see, only just those things you can definitely recognise, such as the rocks around you or the next rise in the ground.

During the course of this second day I decided I should be forced to give myself up as I could not go far in any case with my ankle in the state it was, and anyhow I reckoned one more day would be the absolute limit. I therefore threw away as much of my pack as I could do without, finally disposing of my revolver and ammunition.

By nightfall I estimated I was still 4 or 5 marches from a line of sandy barren hills which I took to be the sand dunes overlooking the sea, and in this estimate I was probably about right as I afterwards heard. I lay down to sleep in a patch of delightfully soft sand after three mouthfulls of water and 3 Horlicks tablets. This was at 10 o'clock in the light of a full moon. In passing, a word about taking nourishment when water is scarce. After a time there is so little saliva that when you attempt to suck a sweet or tablet it will only dissolve with the heat of the body and not in the normal way with the effect of the saliva: at the end of this second day, I just couldn't get Horlicks tablets to dissolve, so I took a very wee sip of water and forced it backwards and forwards through my teeth while *sucking tablets. This eventually made a strong solution of Horlicks milk and went down well, leaving the mouth reasonably refreshed as well.*

A Diesel lorry drove by soon after I had laid down and other traffic was passing too, close by where I was. I checked up and found my water was nearly gone and it seemed I must be right on the coast road. Then there was my Crew who had been faced with 30 miles of desert and no water or rations. I knew I could not last much longer and 10 to 1 the others would be hard put to it, so I gave myself up to a passing car which had 3 Germans on board.

22ⁿᵈ *September 1942*

My captor turned out to be a Warrant Officer or equivilant. He sat behind me grimly clutching his Hauser automatic and likewise his Pal in the back seat. They gave me unsweetened black coffee (The Huns only drink) and offered me food. I tried their biscuits, but, was quite unable to swallow them no matter how I chewed them up. A little brown bread and bully fared no better simply turning to a leathery mass in my mouth. That day I just drank endless cups of coffee (water being aparantly unobtainable) and ate practically nothing until evening.

I was first taken into Tobruk to an Army (or Airforce) H.Q. in the YMCA building, but, at both this and another H.Q. near by they were not interested and I was taken out to El Gubi Aerodrome to await developments.

The Huns were good to me, taking me into their mess and giving me a lot of the eternal black coffee – I'd have given anything for a pint or two of honest to goodness water. I also managed a bit of sausage.

That morning an Officer was introduced to me as one of the Flak Blokes and he was very interested in my downfall – could it be in any way due to his efforts? I replied that I appreciated his thirst for knowledge but I was not prepared to divulge in any way the cause of my forced landing.

That afternoon an escorting Officer was found to see me on the way to Fula in a TV52: this trip in common with all others was done at nought feet.

Nothing of any consequence happened here, they gave me stew for supper and very good it was too, and a liberal portion of cheap red wine and so to bed. To bed with armed guards either end of the tent. The R.A.F. were raiding nearby, but not near enough to effect us and we slept soundly. Talking of drink, it seemed the Luftwaft do not have a bar in any of their messes in the desert and in fact they never drink except for the rare and very odd bottle of cheap red wine. There is a curious herbal tea which tastes like nothing on earth, otherwise it is black coffee or nothing.

23rd September 1942

At about 10.30 my escort bundled me into the back of a Fiesler Storch and we were flown to a minute L.G. near El Daba. This turned out to be the initial interrogation place, but, they got but little out of me except that I did declare the place we had come down and asked for a search to be made. This they said they had done later, but, anyhow as it was four days after the episode it was hardly likely to produce results.

They treated me well at Daba giving me a pair of Battle Dress trousers and letting me bathe in the sea. The sea bathing was however not so good as it was somewhat rough and very rocky and I could not cope at all well on my ropey leg.

That evening there was quite a scene in my tent when a very rough Hun came in and shouted some unintelligible word at me a number of times. It had something to do with trousers: I just could not understand until at last it was evident I had to give up not only my trousers, but, every thing I wore below the waist: boots, stockings, pants and shorts and all the lot. The cause of stringency of this rule was not at the time apparent: I took it to be because of the very poor fence of barbed wire and gerneral lack of security, but, subsequently learnt they had only recently had to deal with an escape.

24th and 25th September, 1942

These two days were quite uneventful. Sgt. Barber a W.T. Op shot down at Tobruk and Sgt. Anson an Army bloke taken on the El Amia line came in and relieved the monotony somewhat, although we weren't permitted to say much to one another.

At least I heard that Dwyer of Wardleys Crew was safe and so was Sgt. Greenstein my Navigator. Sgt. Barber and Anson left in the early hours of 25th (a.m.) and I left 24 hours later at about 4 o'clock in the a.m. on the 26th September 1942.

We met again in Athens a few days later incidentally. The food was passable though thrown at one in any old tin. The bread in ME is exactly the same as anywhere else – a whole-meal job not unlike ours and a thoroughly wholesome article. Their margarine is often of a most peculiar type, being for all the world like cart grease, but, better than nothing on otherwise dry bread. I could not acustom myself to their way of having one big meal comprising an enormous bowl of anything the Cook could lay his hands on. I could not eat more than a quarter of it; I couldn't even if I'd liked it: there just isn't room in my system – the Hun must be developing a ruminant stomach it seems!

26th September, 1942
My last day in Africa, though I did not know it till some time after leaving Daba. Up at 3.30 a.m. and off to an Aerodrome 8 or 10 miles south of Fuua where we enplaned on a 52 for El Gubi. I was given a sack containing 2 loaves and 2 tins for rations, not to forget the inevitable bottle of black coffee sans sugar. The early morning coastal fog was thick in patches and might have afforded a brief spell off freedom if not a get away, but, I could not possibly run for it.

At Tobruk I saw a number of Sikh P.O.W.'s who had been taken at Mera Matruh in the last push. One of them spoke to me and gave me a cup of water – I felt very sorry for them. The Germans treated them like dirt.

One of the Battery Commanders took me in to his Mess while we waited for the 52's from Crete or wherever they were coming from. Once again I failed to enlighten my Host just why I had fallen into Hun Hands, but, he was most kind to me and gave me a huge handfull of sweets and twenty Gold Band cigarettes (one of the best German brands and very nice too). He and another German Officer discussed this and that with me. As so many others had said 'If only you and we could go together, the whole world would be ours' or words to that effect. I could not seem to make them understand that the British don't want the whole world. One thing: on a hint from me about the Stalias and their shortcomings they said

'Oh! But you have your Allies too.' They were refering to the Russians: I did not think it policy to argue the point as I should have got not a little heated if I had. They hate the Russians, they say they are BEASTS, they are not civilised.... and so on. The worthy Battery Commander was a typical Hun – overflowing with confidence in his own ability and filled right up to the back teeth with Propaganda and – in a word 'all his thinking done for him!'

One point about the Hun Officers Mess and one presumes the same applies to the men: The highly efficient Air Service to Africa includes a vast quantity of literature, mostly overflowing with lurid war pictures, and in this way their Forces are kept up to date with the latest news which the ever watchful Goebels permits to come across.

At 3.30 p.m. that afternoon (26th September) I was on board a JU52 taxying to the down wind side of El Gubi Aerodrome. The motors were stopped and we waited for the zero time. Zero hour arrived, motors started, no running up, just off we go – 12 JU52's in a nondescript formation at Nil feet heading for Crete and for a time, two JU88's accompanied us, but, I could not be absolutely sure of the details as I could not really see a lot out of my window, looking into the sun.

That evening we touched down at Malemi just before dark. Malemi is not a large aerodrome by any means and it is very dusty. Those Hun Pilots certainly handled their 52's very nicely, putting them down one after the other in nice precision except for one.

As he parachuted out of the Wimpey Roger became a member of the Caterpillar club.

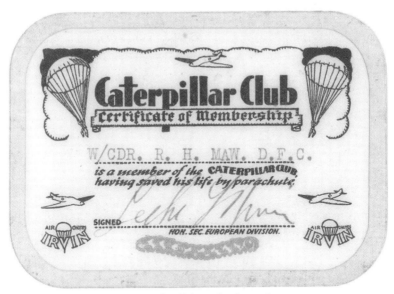

Caterpillar Club membership card

MIDDLE EAST COMMAND
EGYPT

The following extracts are from a Combined Situation Report.

20 Sept.
At night. Wellingtons bombed TOBRUK Harbour but results were obscured by low cloud. 1 Wellington is missing.

Bostons attacked enemy aircraft on a landing ground W. of EL DHABA. Fires and explosions were caused.

Hurricanes machine-gunned M.T. and camps E. of EL DHABA. A vehicle was destroyed and a number of fires were started.

21 Sept.
Fighters destroyed 1 Me. 109 over the battle area and damaged 1 Ju.88 W. of the DELTA.

21 Sept.
Owing to adverse weather only 10 A/S sorties were flown.

STALAG LUFT III

Stalag Luft

My wings are clipped, I languish here,
A human bird within a cage,
It does no good imprisoned here
To fill my heart with useless rage.

My crew were lost, they burned to death,
Though I was chosen to survive,
I rail at fate with angry breath,
But thank my God I am alive.

The weeks, the months, the years drag by,
And often, in the desolate night,
We hear our bombers in the sky
And pray for them with all our might.

We think of life beyond the wire,
The English spring, the gentle rain,
The village church with slender spire,
The honeysuckle in the lane.

Our hearts are filled with longing for
Those dear ones whom we cannot see,
The home, the garden, sea and shore,
The city streets, the Christmas tree.

We plan escapes, we play our games,
We read, we learn, we help our friends

With foreign uniforms and names,
Until this cruel warfare ends.

We find that men from many lands
Can breach the gap that language makes,
When mutual suffering joins their hands,
And nations learn from their mistakes.

A noble thought? Yes, that may be,
But we have had to pay the cost
And give, in order to be free,
These precious years of youth we've lost.

The sun is shining, golden, clear,
Upon a sparkling English stream,
It also shines upon us here,
But England still is just a dream.

Audrey Grealy

Roger was not on Crete long, but while there he met an Italian doctor who looked at his ankle, commenting "It's a pity you walked so far on it, but I will see what I can do," which he did. The ankle easier, Roger was moved on via trains and transit camps, with a brief stay in Athens, towards the POW camps in Eastern Germany. Train journeys were either on hard wooden third class benches or 'cattle class' with occasional stops for soup. The train eventually halted at a country station on the main line at Sagan, 90 miles south east of Berlin in the province of Silesia near the old Polish border.

A closely guarded group of unkempt RAF officers were marched from Sagan railway station between tall, dark, forbidding pine trees to the prison gates of Stalag Luft III, a camp designed and run by the Luftwaffe, German Air Force men, many of whom flew in the First World War as had the camp Kommandant Colonel Friedrich von Lindeiner-Wildau. He had been on the personal staff of Goering, also a World War I pilot with some sympathy for flying men.

Roger's first impression was of miles of barbed wire surrounding a barren landscape with large wooden huts on stilts guarded by tall towers with armed sentries and big searchlights.

They shuffled through the gates and stood in rows to be counted and searched again. Then they were officially welcomed by the Senior British Officer and half a dozen others who led them to the nearest hut in the East Compound where they sat down on the floor dejectedly clutching a hot mug of tea. The Senior British Officer gave a short welcome speech expecting that as officers they would do their best to keep fit and smartly turned out, which raised a laugh as he had odd socks on. He introduced the 'Doc' who would attend to any medical problems, then asked their previous occupations, hobbies and skills. Among this group were a violinist, a tailor, an architect and a carpenter who would all prove very useful to the escaping committee.

The Senior British Officer told Roger that as a Wing Commander he was entitled to a two-bunk room but with rank came responsibilities. He would be responsible for the smooth running of the hut and the duty pilot rota. The duty 'pilots' had two-hour shifts in daylight at the library window overlooking the main gate – all comings and goings duly noted in a book. Most of the guards had nicknames – these duty pilot books were so well kept the senior guards would sometimes check on their juniors to see if they arrived on time!

Each of the six-bunk rooms had a senior officer responsible for them, referring sick men to the medics and sorting problems – any too difficult he would refer to the senior officer in charge of the hut.

Roger found out it could be a few weeks before Janett would hear from the Red Cross where he was, but he would be allowed to send two letters and two postcards a month – all censored by the Sagan ladies in the hut at the end of the East Compound. A 'Next of kin parcel' could be sent to him every six months, clothes, soap, chocolate etc but anyone could send cigarettes at duty free prices. The Red Cross parcels would be shared out with the men in his mess.

A Red Cross parcel

Roger was allocated a small room at the end of hut 64 as he was a Wing Commander. He would 'mess' with the six men in the next room sharing food but excused cooking duties by his rank. The German kitchen provided boiling water, collected in jugs, for tea at breakfast time, and some black, soggy sour bread which probably contained some sawdust. The official allowance was one loaf per person per week. At lunchtime Green Death could be collected in jugs – a soup of anything that came to hand. The Red Cross parcels made up for the lack of meat and milk in tins. The Klim (milk spelled backwards) tins were useful for making so many things. There were 'tin bashers' in every hut, they would open both ends of the tin, cut along the seam and roll it flat with a bottle before cutting it to the required shapes. The stove in Roger's mess was small and fuel not too plentiful so he cut flanges of tin attached in a circle which fitted under a kettle to give a quick boiling effect.

Among the men in Roger's 'mess' were Ollie Philpot, Tom Wilson the violinist, and Doug Cooper. The hut had several bunk rooms with Roger's small room one end and the German Supply Officer's room at the other end, next to the night latrine, a necessity as the huts were locked at night.

Typical room in Stalag Luft III

Prisoners cooking meagre rations. Smoking helped to dull hunger pains.

The Prisoner of War

THE OFFICIAL JOURNAL OF THE PRISONERS OF WAR DEPARTMENT OF THE RED CROSS AND ST. JOHN WAR ORGANISATION, ST. JAMES'S PALACE, LONDON, S.W.1

VOL. 2. No. 15   Free to Next of Kin   JULY, 1943

The Editor Writes —

WHEN our prisoners of war get home again they will be eager for information about things which have happened during their absence. Except for scraps of information received in letters, they will have had little news of events in the outside world.

I have often wondered whether any steps could be taken now to help to fill this gap in their lives when they return. And now comes an excellent suggestion from Mrs. V. M. Jones, of Truro, the wife of a prisoner and the mother of two babies.

Her News Scrapbook

She says that every evening she collects all the local papers she can find and cuts out the pictures of the everyday news of the war "so that on my husband's return he can look through these and see how it all went." She adds that it helps her when she is missing him most, which I can well believe. Twice a week she writes to him and every day she adds to her scrapbook. I feel sure that her idea will strongly appeal to many wives and mothers of prisoners-of-war, but I would suggest that anybody starting such a scrapbook should not confine her collection to photographs or to news about the fighting fronts. They will be especially interested in what is happening at home.

Has England Changed ?

I have been reading some very interesting letters from a prisoner of war in Stalag IIID, Works Camp 520, for whom parcels are being sent by a lady who lives in Coventry. It turned out that he belonged to the Coventry squadron of his Yeomanry Regiment and knows Coventry very well. "Poor brave Coventry," he writes, "how glad I'd be to be there again. It seems a lifetime since I left three years ago, but at the same time a bare five minutes. Did you hear Paul Robeson when he sang at the Hippodrome one Sunday night?" And again : "Receiving mail is the chief excitement of this life. . . . Do not feel too sorry for us. We do not do at all badly. It takes quite a lot to bother us, provided we know that all's well at home. . . . How much has England changed since '39, I wonder? It is so easy to imagine things just as they were, that there

Air Force prisoners—an informal group at Stalag Luft 3.

will probably be a big surprise for all of us in the changes."

Unimagined Blessings

Corporal W. E. Sprake has spontaneously addressed an eloquent postcard to the British Red Cross Society to express "something of the appreciation which we Gefangeners really feel about the truly wonderful work your Society is doing and has done for us and our people at home." He talks of their existence being converted into "even a pleasurable life," thanks not only to the food supplies generously supplied. "Little did we think," he concludes, "in our early days at Corinth that such blessings as we now have could ever be."

"I'll Never Pass a Box By"

A similar tribute comes to hand in a letter to Mrs. Katherine Flack of Aberdare, from her husband in another Stalag : "They are grand people, these Red Cross, and I'll never pass a box by when I get home—no, sir, God knows how we would have got on without them." Such letters as these, and we get many, are highly prized by all of us in Red Cross and St. John who are taking part in the work for prisoners-of-war. I quote from one or two of them occasionally, more especially to show those who make our work possible, the public who supply the funds, how greatly their generosity is appreciated.

Easter Day in Stalag 383

From a letter of a sergeant in Stalag 383 (formerly Oflag IIIC) to his wife at Stalbridge (Dorset), I get an account of

POW 'newspaper' sent to relations

Janett was desperate for news of Roger, she had the 'your husband is missing' letter and wrote immediately to Wing Commander Gibson now in charge of 108 Squadron in the desert. He replied that Roger was a prisoner of war in Germany but he knew nothing about the crew, and as she had requested sent her the names and addresses of all their next of kin. Janett lost no time writing and eventually was able to put a tick by each name as they all survived baling out in the desert.

Roger was pleased to find a camp 'newspaper' pinned on each hut notice board with surprisingly accurate accounts of the war on all its fronts. He was able to read an old one about the battle of El Alamein and delighted at the outcome. The illicit radios and the German-speaking POWs were pretty accurate news suppliers. He was pleased too that Janett would be receiving a POW 'newspaper' with articles from the many POW camps in Eastern Germany.

Officers were not expected to work and appell was only called twice a day when the prisoners went outside on parade to be counted which would take about half an hour, so there was plenty of time for talk, clubs, creative hobbies, reading, and writing letters. Several men studied for exams and there was a lot of sport, football, rugby, cricket, volleyball, softball and boxing. Some men even made a rough golf course, and in the winter the Canadians flooded the football pitch to freeze for ice hockey.

Roger soon settled into camp life as he had been at boarding school in the First World War with poor food, cold baths, arctic dormitories and writing home on Sunday. He met several men from his former 12 Squadron at Binbrook and a reunion was held complete with photograph from a camera someone had acquired from one of the guards.

Ex 12 Squadron reunion, Stalag Luft III, late 1942. Roger standing second left.

Roger heard about Douglas Bader's brief stay at the camp – he had parachuted out of a burning fighter plane leaving one of his artificial legs which was trapped behind. The Germans gave permission for a new leg to be flown in and delivered by parachute. His wife had packed the hollow leg with all his favourite tobacco and chocolate. The Germans were sure he would try to escape so they moved him on to Colditz under heavily armed guard which he found very amusing, pretending to 'inspect' the 70 armed men, giving his bag to one to carry.

Stalag Luft III opened in April 1942, Roger arrived in the autumn and by then 60 or 70 tunnels had been discovered and there were many other escapes tried, men disguised, and walking out of the gates, hiding in laundry and rubbish carts, all ending at pistol point and marched to the 'cooler', a small unheated cell for 10 days.

There were so many British and American airmen parachuting out over Germany that a large new compound was being built to the North, which meant rich picking opportunities to bribe the Russian prisoners working on the site with cigarettes in exchange for offcuts of wood and small tools. Roger's little room grew more littered by the day. Having no other Wing Commander to share with, the bottom bunk contained his 'nest' of the regulation two thin blankets sewn together and filled with newspaper for added insulation. The top bunk was a masterful collection of 'come in usefuls' scrounged over time. Klim tins in rows on wooden shelves, in disorderly confusion under the bed, and on the table and chairs – each holding nails, screws, bits of glass, paint from the theatre, bits of string, wire, and many other things. On the top bunk lay a broken ukele, part of a cast iron stove, a wooden bicycle partly made and 'spare' bed boards, no longer needed as the bed now had a string/rope hammock bottom not unlike the Indian charpoys, with a bit of cardboard for added insulation.

THE CLOCK

Almost as soon as I arrived at Sagan, I decided to turn my hand to some form of wood work or 'Tin bashing'. Above all I felt the need for something to take my mind away from the inevitable present.

Some of my fellow unfortunates were making, or had made model boats. I heard tales of steam engines that worked and many ingenious ideas, but the one which took my fancy was a clock: I could get no information about it except that it worked and could be seen in the next compound. I did see it eventually but not for some time and then not in detail.

I knew nothing whatever about clocks and nobody else seemed to either, so there were bound to be plenty of failures, and much time would (or could) evidently be wiled away: besides it did'nt (sic) matter in the least if it never worked. So that is how it all started.

THE FIRST DESIGN

After swinging a stone on a bit of Red Cross string and contemplating the mystic symbols $T = 2\pi\sqrt{l/g}$, and at the same time trying to visualise a Grandfather Clock, a muddled idea became upermost (sic) in my mind that a good start would be to cater for an escapement doing about 30 swings per minute. One snag at this early stage was that 'T' never seemed to equal $2\pi\sqrt{l/g}$ or $2\pi\sqrt{}$ anything else, and anyway who ever contemplated such trivialities when setting out to make a clock of old tins?

So a start was made. A sheet of drawing paper was procured and a train of gears designed to provide three four to one increases from the main to the escapement shafts: that is 64 to 1, or 64 revolutions of the escapement wheel per hour (in theory).

For no apparent reason 12 spoke lantern pinions and 48 tooth spur wheels were chosen for this part of the works, and it is interesting to note that I descovered (sic) much later a ten tooth lantern Pinion is regarded as the smallest practical size.

After much cutting up of old butter tins, the first train of gears was at last mounted, and the whole terminated in an escapement which was evidently never going to function. This work occupied some five or six months off and on.

Before leaving this first stage, it may be mentioned the gear train was complete, including a friction drive and standard reduction between the minute and hour hands, the former being mounted direct on the main shaft. The time drive wheel was mounted on and fixed to the main shaft. This wheel had a clutch face of beechwood, built integral with it and was driven by the other face of the clutch. The other or rear face of the clutch was integral with the first spur wheel and was lose on the main shaft: the drive between the two clutch faces was acquired by the end pressure of a light involute spring on the rear of the main shaft.

THE ESCAPEMENT

The first design for the Escapement wheel comprised a 30 tooth wheel built up of two tin discs either side of a beechwood boss, with boot tacks riveted between the discs. Nothing was known about, or could in any way be found out about standard escapement designs until long after the work had been under way, when Flt Jacoby came on the scene: in fact the whole idea had been shelved, pending inspiration and the necessary urge. Jacoby was a plump and jovial Officer, extreemly (sic) fond of music and very clever with watches, this being his profession. He described the basic principles of an escapement design which was adopted and which worked first time.

As a matter of interest, the first abortive attempt was a shot at 'So-and so's Dead-beat Escapement', and in principal the design was almost dead right, even down to the number of teeth in the wheel: but as already intimated, it had prooved (sic) just about as 'dead-beat' as one could possibly have hoped for.

THE DRIVE AND FINAL MODIFICATIONS

Initial experiments with the new Escapement proved that the best rate of swing of the pendulum appeared to necessitate an additional 3 to 1 gear beyond the existing train, but further tests finally settled this last ratio at 2:1. The final ratio therfore (sic) became 128:1, which with the new escapement necessitated timing to 64 swings per minute of the Pendulum.

The original drive was intended to be by sprocket and chain, but a short length of chain was tried and prooved (sic) a failure owing to inaccuracy and excessive friction, besides the excessive weight on the main shaft. A considerable modification was then evolved: this consisted of a drum at the side of the clock, which drove the first spur wheel through a free wheel and 32 tooth Lantern Pinion.

The winding mechanism simply consisted of a square end on the drum shaft and a key rather like an Austen (sic) Seven crank handle: this item was cast in Zink (sic) and inserted through a hole in the clock face when required. The original driving medium was short lengths of catgut or Hun boot lace: later on a much better driving twine was made by twisting six strands of good thread into a single continuous well waxed cord.

FINAL ADJUSTMENTS

From re-commencing work on the new Escapement and additional gears to final completion of the case occupied a further 7 or 8 months: the Clock ran very well for some time, after which it gave trouble and was left for a further period until the necessary urge for more work should be forthcomming. When this happened, a new set of gears were designed and built between the fourth shaft and the escapement: this was the final form of the works and it ran much better, being adjustable for timing to within two minutes in 12 hours.

The time cannot be re-set in the normal way as the minute hand would split or at least very soon loosen on its shaft, so a large hole is provided in the clock base to enable the intermediate gear in the hand drive to be pushed round with the fore finger.

MATEREALS USED

This final paragraph indicates the parts of the Clock and the matereals from which they were made:

DRIVING MECHANISM - *Drum of wood with beechwood inset for free wheel drive at front end. Drum Axel, leg of a steel music stand: this axel runs in bearings cast from an old Zink (sic) Basin.*

SPUR WHEELS - *These are of standard design and consist of two sheets of tin riveted together with boot nails and with a sheet of stiff card board between.*

LANTERN PINIONS - *These are built up with tin end plates and wooden hubs: the spokes are soft Iron wire from Hun cheese boxes.*

AXELS - *The driving drum Axel, as already mentioned is part of an old music stand. The acquisition of this entailed a certain amount of friction with the Camp Band Drummer who became placated after receiving a soft Iron wire job in lieu.*

The main axel is a coat hangar hook, straightened out as nearly as possible.

The Escapement Axel is part of the winding handle of a disused Gramaphone.

All the other Axels are made of wire from a certain type of lamp bracket provided by a greatful Hun Government.

ESCAPEMENT & PENDULUM - The tickers or 'Pallets' are brass from a mouth organ and are soldered onto the extremities of a pair of tin plates which form the rocker arm. This assembly is attached at its centre to a brass dart which serves for the Rocker Arm Axel.

The Pendulum is suspended on two short lengths of watch spring. The Pendulum itself is of wood, terminating in a Zink (sic) casting supported over an adjusting nut.

The Zink (sic) was melted down from an old basin and the adjusting screw started life on a banjo.

BEARINGS - Two double thickness channel section tin plates are arranged front and back of the clock and serve for most of the bearings. The Main Shaft bearings are re-enforced with brass from a mouth Organ and those of the main Drum are Zink (sic) castings. The hour hand drive, which is integral with a 48 tooth Spur Wheel and rotating freely on the minute hand or main shaft is a silver paper casting.

DRIVING WEIGHT - A Concrete weight with removable wooden block for the pulley wheel was cast for the original drive, but the wooden block can easily be lashed to a brick, a lump of coal, old boot or any suitable weight. The weight is approximately 3000 grammes (about 6½ lbs). With a single pulley, a weight drop of six feet gives roughly 14 hours run.

CLOCK CASE
The case is made up from odds and ends of old Red Cross Packing cases.

The curved sides are a single ply of 3 ply from a Canadian Red Cross Crate. The face is veneered with wood taken from two cheap Ukulele Cases which had providentially been broken in the post. The hands and figures (or rather letters) on the Clock Face are carved in Oak and inlaid: the oak for this purpose was cut from a board intended for coat hangar pegs.

The clock face

The tiny wood burning stove was a great asset but if it was going all night to stop him freezing, Roger found it was too stuffy in the morning so the stove was well stoked at lights out, the window open a bit and at 3 a.m. the clock triggered a violent reaction with the weight hurtling down and shutting the window – unfortunately on the initial run his crockery was in the way on the window ledge!

New pilots were arriving all the time and Roger Bushell, son of a mining engineer joined them in the autumn of 1942. This charismatic fighter pilot was a great boost to the escaping committee, he just looked a the 14 foot high double fence with coils of barbed wire in between and started thinking. The 'trip' wire was just inside the fence next to the perimeter track that everyone walked round each day for exercise. The Germans would shoot if anyone stepped over it.

Stalag Luft III was built as an escape proof camp. Huts on stilts so any tunnelling would be noticed immediately The under layer of sand was a different colour to the top layer so that would be obvious too, and difficult to dispose of. There were German guards who marched on sentry duty with loaded guns and manned the towers, mostly older men not needed at the Russian front, the prisoners called them Goons. The main danger to escapees were the 'ferrets', Germans who infiltrated the camp, they might come hidden in a laundry truck and crawl under huts looking for signs of tunnels, listening to conversations, crawling in the roof spaces – dangerous men, even the Goons did not know where they all were.

Three Goons – a drawing by Jill Bennett

Roger had an unfortunate run in with a ferret. He had designed and built an air conditioning/cooling system, cutting a hole in the floor for cool air to come in propelled by a home-made fan – wooden blades fitted onto a wheel, driven by a shaft running up to a workbench with a broken gramophone on top. When he turned the gramophone handle the fan revolved drawing in cool air from below. Unfortunately a ferret found it by crawling underneath and started to block up the hole – Roger stamped his trap door shut on the unsuspecting fingers and was off to the cooler for another 28 days. Injuring an officer of the Third Reich was a serious offence and the whole camp speculated on the outcome. When he was released they all thought he would go back after a day so his friend thoughtfully provided him with a good seat in the theatre at the pantomime Red Riding Hood – it was a great production, the over-large fairy 'fell' through the stage (another trap door) and an Australian known as Bookie Bob came on stage to auction Cell 4 in the cooler for one night only, inviting bets from the audience who erupted with laughter.

Christmas was approaching, the Red Cross parcels got through. Some had been keeping raisins aside for a cake and some for the still which bubbled away day and night in one of the huts. It was a creative design made of some 'acquired' plumbing and one or two wind instruments, producing enough almost pure alcohol for several people to ignore the pain of hunger and missing Christmas at home completely for almost 24 hours. The German guards turned a blind eye to it, welcoming the brief warmth of the hut from their guard duties as they brought their bottles and 'pay' which could be anything the prisoners needed from food to razor blades. One time Roger and Doug Cooper were making a hidey hole in the still room and a guard walked past them noticing nothing but the bubbling twice distilled liquor. At midnight on Christmas Eve the snowy starlit silence was broken by a lone trumpeter playing Silent Night, both British and German voices joined in.

Roger's room at the end of Block 64 overlooked the central open space of the camp where the German loudspeaker was mounted. They switched it on at 6 a.m. for a Physical Exercise programme, all in German with loud invigorating music. Roger protested bitterly against this. When he was asleep he claimed he was free. By being woken up two hours too early he was being subjected to 14 hours extra captivity per week, 30 whole days a year which was surely against the Geneva Convention. He took this

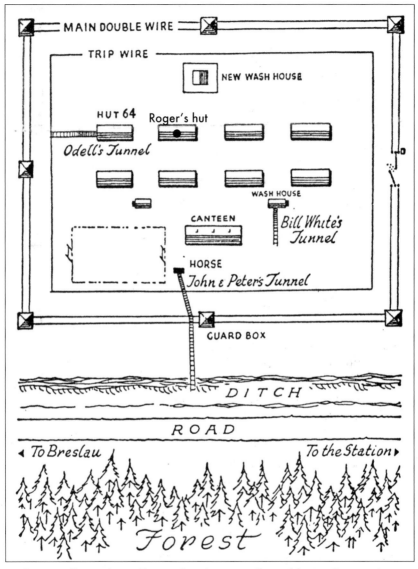

Diagram of layout of camp. This area forms but one small part of the overall camp and was situated in the South East corner.

complaint to the German officer at the other end of his hut with several other 'supporters' forming a ragged queue. The officer frequently left his key in the lock, and while Roger was in full flow one of the 'supporters' removed the key and made an impression in a block of soap, from which a good key was eventually made so they always had access to the 'Verboten' room. Roger won his point and the loudspeaker was silent until 8 a.m. so mornings could begin more peacefully with the man on mess duty putting tea in a jug and taking it to the German cookhouse for boiling water. Every morning began the same, he gently rocked the grey bundle on Roger's bed, "Morning Harry". A hand would emerge from the cocoon on the bottom bunk and withdraw the precious mug, first to be cradled as a hot water bottle, then sipped slowly in appreciation.

When meals were ready it was important to serve them straightaway. Wings (Maw) was always absorbed in one task or another so a whistle was acquired and hung on the back of the door to summon him – it was known as 'Wing's whistle' and someone had written 'penalty for improper use – 20 points'!

Letters were getting through now and his father's letters always stamped 'write legibly to avoid delay' were all of farming, the crops, familiar field names and a wistful query if Roger might one day become a 'son of the soil'. Some lines were blue inked out as the Sagan interpreter ladies had thought it might be a code, but Janett's cheerful 'your cousin Winston is very well' was usually left alone. With Janett's letter in May came the saddest of news that her beloved brother Maurice had been killed in Tunisia. A parcel arrived from Cleatham, a large fruit cake, socks, several goodies lovingly packed and four precious photos, one of his father (over 6 foot tall) standing in a field of rye – a bumper crop shoulder high.

By now Roger's room (12 foot by 6 foot) was almost a proper workshop with a workbench and drawing board under the window and tools in orderly racks. The tools on display were cunningly made of cardboard and scraps of wood covered with silver paper from cigarette packets. Regular snap raids by the ferrets were made and growls of annoyance at their 'finds'. His real tools – the big saw which he could only use when the guards were the other end of the camp and others made or acquired were securely hidden in hidey holes, the best of which was in the German officer's hut, behind his chair at the other end of the hut where they kept

Father by the rye crop

Arthur, Lucy, Emma and Skipworth in Cleatham garden

the fake passports, papers and keys, compasses and maps. Several of his friends remember holding the 'fat' lamp and handing tools and screws as he carefully removed some groove and tongue pine board from its place in the hut wall and replacing it ready for use, invisible to most people.

During May 1943 came the incredible news of the destruction of the dams in the Ruhr valley by Barnes Wallis's bouncing bombs dropped by Lancaster bombers. Details of the raid took up most of Alan Mackay's

The prize winning Shires and their latest foals

'The Daily Recco' which he claimed was the only free press in Nazi-occupied Europe.

Roger's 'Next of kin' parcel contained a pair of Ethie's best socks – Janett's mother was always knitting – precious photos of Mike and Joshey.

Mike

Joshey

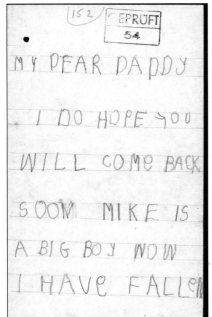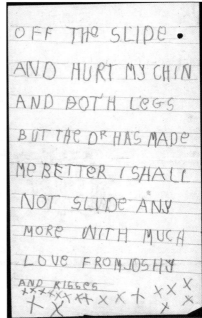

Letter from Joshey

The model yacht on the drawing board was making progress onto the bench, it was clinker built with narrow planks cut carefully from cigar boxes, a masterpiece for Mikey. The rigging was almost complete when there was a knock on the door, Ollie Philpot and Eric Williams with an IDEA. Checking for listening ferrets, they outlined the plan of a vaulting horse – or box – strong enough to carry a man, which would be set down on the same spot each day near the wire fence so a 'moler' tunnel could be made underneath. Roger drew on a piece of paper, it must be light but very strong. Making sure Roger Bushell, the escape officer, knew of the plan, Roger's only concern was to find the materials. The roof above his room was already weakened by removal of 'non essential' timber and most of his bed boards had gone to various projects, but with diligent scrounging and Red Cross parcel plywood for covering from Roger's secret store the IDEA became a reality. Most of it could be made in full view of the Germans, sewing the padded top out in the June sunshine. Vaulters were called for and rose to the challenge, barefoot as no-one had gym shoes. At first there was one man who pretended to fail, knocking the box over, and the bored German guards on the towers enjoyed the

179

spectacle, viewing the empty 'horse' and waiting each time to laugh at the unfortunate.

Vaulting over 'The horse'

As days went by the vaulters got better, this was when Roger supplied hooks to the inside of the top of the horse to hold tools and sand bags. The digger would ride on the two long poles put through the holes either side to carry it in and out of the hut.

The horse stood 4 feet 6 inches high, the base covering an area 5 feet by 3 feet. The sides tapered up to the top made of bed boards, padded with straw from mattresses and covered in the white canvas which cigarettes had travelled in from Turkey. The 6 foot pieces of 3 by 2 inch ex roof rafters made the handles for four men when put through the carrying holes. The horse was kept in a long low extension to the camp kitchen in a large empty room used by the orchestra and choir to practice in. The entrance was double doors above a flight of steps.

Carrying 'The horse'

Digger emerging with sandbags

181

Posters were made and put up round the camp advertising gym classes in vaulting, and German speakers spoke casually to guards about this latest keep fit craze.

The horse was placed 45 feet from the trip wire, adding tunnel length for the wire itself and a danger zone outside the tunnel would come to about 115 feet. The vaulters dug two sand pits to lessen the shock of landing in bare feet on the baked earth, these were good markers to put the horse down in the exact position each time. Many prisoners cut off trouser legs in the hot summer, with some stitching they made ideal sand bags. The tunneller sat on one of the carrying poles, feet braced each side on the bottom framework, he carried a Red Cross cardboard box with the trouser legs and the hooks. Once in position he worked quickly to put the grey surface sand into the box and fill the sand bags with a stolen bricklayer's trowel, and start shoring up the tunnel entrance. He put a plywood sheet over the hole, then standing on the framework of the horse he carefully spread sand over it, packing it down hard and covering it with the grey sand. Sweating and exhausted he called softly that he had finished – the rafter poles were re-inserted and the horse carried back to the canteen.

Disposing of the yellow sand was not easy, 'penguin men' carried long sausages of sand made from arms and legs of winter underwear slung round their necks and down their trouser legs. Some sand was worked into the little gardens, some into the latrines, some buried under huts. When they reached the bottom of the shaft another raid was made on the unfinished bath house for bricks and the tunnel entrance was covered each time with sand bags, then yellow sand firmly packed before the grey sand.

While the tunnel grew inch by inch, day by day, the escape committee were working flat out – often at night when the doors were locked until lights out, to produce civilian clothes, maps and documents. Compasses were made by heating broken gramophone records over boiling water, cutting circles with a homemade tin pastry cutter and fashioned into a small round container, complete with a gramophone needle and part of a razor blade that had been magnetized by putting a bunch of them in the electric wire junction, blacking out the camp and upsetting the guards considerably.

As Roger was with Ollie every meal time he was aware of his meticulous preparations for escape. His passport and papers would show Jon Jörgensen, a Norwegian businessman, he had spent some time in Norway early on after his capture. Ollie 'visited Dean and Dawson' the 'travel agents' of Stalag Luft III who would prepare his papers using the German eagle stamp cut from the head of a shoe repair kit.

Permit to travel

Name __Van Damme Willy.__

(surname   first name)

Born on __1. June 1905__   in __Bruges, Belgium__

Place of residence __Brussels, Belgium__

Profession __Electrician__

is permitted to travel between __23. June 1943__ and __29. June 1943__

from __Leipzig__ to __Danzig__

purpose __To carry out electrical work in the__

__dockyard__

Signed __G. Schmidt__

Chief of Police, Leipzig

Official stamp

Date __20. June 1943__

Model of a permit

Maps were studied and train timetables. His clothes were as smart as wartime and the camp tailors could manage, civilian buttons, even German shoe laces as Hitler Youth would be everywhere eagle-eyed for tell-tale details. He would cut his moustache on the day of the escape.

Ollie's cover was to be a margarine salesman, carrying a new super food (a block of escapers cake) which he covered in a Danzig margarine wrapper. If asked he would say his firm was producing it to give the Germans more energy to fight the Bolsheviks. One of Ollie's worries was his second set of papers showing him to be a Swedish sailor and listing his recent ships in case he was caught in a harbour looking for a ship to stow away on. Roger designed and made a wooden presentation case for the 'super food', complete with false bottom for the 'sailor's papers'. This was packed beside his clean shirt and collars, German razor and soap in the small attaché case which had British Made carefully painted over. Ollie told Roger he must take his identity disc with him so if things went badly he could prove he was British. He hid it between two layers of cardboard with a picture of his wife stuck to it so that it looked like a keepsake hung round his neck.

Next lunchtime Roger was amazed to see Ollie (a non-smoker) struggling to light a pipe – he thought it would give him time to stop and look at street signs or station information without appearing too suspicious.

The tunnel was taking much longer than they had calculated but the horse was holding up well to such heavy use inside and out. The escape committee gave extra food to the tunnellers, but the vaulters were getting tired. Tom Wilson tore his Achilles tendon on landing, so his role now one of 'lookout', using his violin practice as a genuine reason to be in the room overlooking the circuit. If Les Sidwell walking the circuit noticed anything suspicious, like ferrets advancing, or a guard using his binoculars too long he would adjust his hat and Tom would change the tune, so any dispersal of sand, tailoring or travel agent work was quickly covered up.

Soon the last Friday in October came. On the first vaulting session Michael Codner was entombed alone in the tunnel. His absence at appell covered by a senior officer who was sick in bed one moment and magically on the end of the parade line the next. The next vaulting session was after appell and three men were carried out in the horse.

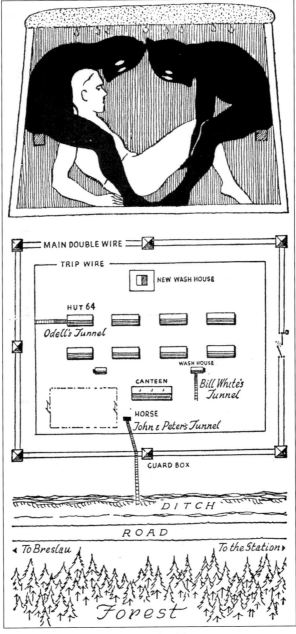

'The horse' the night of the escape

185

Ollie and Eric completely covered in darkly dyed Red Cross underwear over their civilian clothes. Freddie McKay to wish them well and seal the tunnel, so they could go on tunnelling past the shored up bit through the 'mole' sand towards the forest and break out under the cover of darkness to go their separate ways.

As they were going to bed that night extra guards marched into camp, photographic 'Goons' came round to each Block with identity cards checking who was present. When they got to Eric and Michael's Block Wing Commander Collard short circuited the electric supply blowing all the fuses. The Goons failed to restore the lights and marched off. When they had left the camp the lights came on again to their anger and disgust.

The remaining prisoners were as Roger put it 'on the crest of no ordinary wave'. In spite of sentries, guards, ferrets, barbed wire, watch towers, floodlights and microphones buried beneath the wire three prisoners had left the 'Escape Proof Camp'.

Next morning at appell the fun began. The Goons were still trying to establish if any prisoners were missing or if they were hiding somewhere in the camp. It was a cold day and the waiting men were restless as the Germans counted, conferred, and recounted. Eventually they set up a line of guards with rifles and bayonets across the parade ground, counted prisoners on one side, uncounted the other. Someone produced a football ,which was kicked quietly one to another until it shot through the front rank to the middle of the parade ground. Someone ran after it and the Lageroffizier, a Hungarian Major, who had been a POW in World War I shouted 'arrest that ball'. It was a farce, the young guard uncertain how to handle gun and bayonet while chasing a football did his best, only to find the ball kicked over his head every time he got near. Then Wing Commander Collard walked through the cordon and challenged Roger – 'Bet your chaps can't score a try behind our lines'. Roger's hut surged forward sweeping through the guards, passing the ball rugger-fashion. Block 68 surged towards them tackling most unfairly anyone with the ball or without. The checked and unchecked inextricably mixed up. It was as the Kommandant later said foolhardy, they could all have been shot. The Hungarian Major marched his men off and the British were returned to their huts, they had given the three escapers a little more precious time.

Soon a large force of Luftwaffe troops was seen marching towards the camp, 50 corporals with Tommy guns leading, backed up by seemingly hundreds of airmen with rifles and bayonets at the sloped arms position. Once in the camp they broke ranks and rushed into every hut firing in the air, pushing the prisoners out onto the parade ground. Prisoners were checked where they stood, the process seemed interminable. Finally, the count complete, the Kommandant announced his displeasure which was translated by his security officer.

From now on you will have three appells a day, cheering from the prisoners. You will be locked in your barracks at 5 p.m. each evening. Hooray they shouted. The YMCA cinema projector will not be permitted here.

The next day was Sunday, church in the theatre was well-attended with its strong choir, and in the afternoon an early performance of French without Tears by Terence Rattigan in the theatre. The following day Group Captain Kellett, the Senior British Officer received the following letter:

Stalag Luft 3.
Kommandantur.   Sagan, 1st November
To the Senior British Officer,
East Camp.
Group Captain R. KELLETT.

In connection with the incidents on Saturday, 30th October 1943, the S.B.O. G/C R. Kellett asked the Kommandant for an interview for him and Group Captain Willetts. The Kommandant also ordered the following six officers Ps.O.W. from the East Camp to be present:-

W/Cdr.	R. COLLARD	P.O.W. No. 568	S.L.3	
W/Cdr.	R. MAW	''	740	''
P/O	W. POULTON	''	207	''
P/O	A. RUFFEL	''	3792	Ofl.XC
P/O	J. WALTERS		714	S.L.2
1st/Lt.	G. HALLER		1424	Ofl.IX A

The Kommandant then made the following statement which was translated into English by Major Dr. Simoleit.

'On the morning of Saturday, 30th October, 1943, incidents took place in the East Camp which could easily have led to very serious consequences. The cause of these incidents was that the Ps.O.W. did not behave in the manner which must be required of them.

My soldiers do not tolerate provocative and mocking behaviour. On Saturday, the German soldiers showed extraordinary self-control when they were greeted as they marched into the camp with extremely improper shouts. Certain Ps.O.W. tried to mock us on our own soil. This behaviour shows a totally wrong-headed outlook. I expect neither liking nor sympathy, but I do expect a military bearing, and respect for German soldiers and for the German uniform. In his own mind, each one of you may think as he likes, but in his behaviour he must conduct himself respectfully and in accordance with his circumstances.

I cannot understand how Senior Staff Officers can encourage their junior comrades to play football during Appel or to run across the Parade Ground from one block to another. W/Cdrs. Collard and Maw may hate us Germans and our country as much as they like, that does not interest me in the slightest: I do not seek their friendship, nor do I need it. But while they are Prisoners of War they will learn what we Germans expect, above all from an officer, namely correct, respectful behaviour in accordance with the German ideals of officership.

On Saturday we arrested 7 men who expressed their bravery, their heroism, and their good up-bringing by grinning shouting and whistling. Behaviour of this kind is only possible if their attitude is totally misguided. I believe I can be certain that at least 95% of the officers in this camp have the same officer-like attitude as we have, but a small proportion appear to desire to make the relations between the detaining power and the Ps.O.W. as strained as possible. I wish to warn these gentlemen and to advise them for the last time to avoid stirring up trouble amongst their comrades.

After the attempted escape on Friday, we discovered that the entrance to the tunnel was on the Sports Field in the Golf Course, and that sand had been dispersed on the Golf Course. The tunnel had to be filled in as quickly as possible and the levelling of the ground was absolutely essential in order to maintain security.

I myself saw as we entered Blocks 68 and 69 that the lights were extinguished and that they came on again as we left the barracks. In order to prevent this kind of mockery during the night, I had the light bulbs removed from both barracks.

The escape on Friday took place from the Northern part of the Sports Field between 1920 and 2120 hours. The Ps.O.W. must therefore have been outside the permitted area at this time, having left their barracks by a route not allowed. As a result I must take all Security measures to see that no-one leaves the barracks after dark or climbs out of the windows. I therefore gave the order forbidding all movement outside the barrack blocks after the circuit lighting is switched on, and having the window shutters closed all night.

I will now repeat the quintessence of my remarks:

1.	I urgently advise the avoidance of any stirring up by underhand propaganda on the part of some of the prisoners, and any sympathetic reception of it by the rest.

2.	I expect no sympathy and I will use all the force at my command to ensure that due respect as well as absolute obedience is paid to the Detaining Power and its representatives.

(Signed)	*Von Lindeiner*
	Oberst and Kommandant

Camp life continued under the new restraints, everyone doing their best to keep fit now the vaulting was over. Football was very popular with leagues and good teams and much betting going on – everyone turning out to watch the matches. Roger's team of slightly older men was irreverently known as the Old Buggers.

There was a Red Letter Day when a parcel arrived for Roger and his mess from Sweden. A box of cooking pots and pans, so they knew their Jon Jörgensen and his two companions had made a home run. It was a terrific boost to morale and great encouragement to friends in the North Compound.

CAMP: Stalag Luft III – scene of the Wooden Horse escape. Right, Oliver Philpot with fellow escapees Michael Codner, left, and Eric Williams, centre, after they had arrived safely in Sweden.

How Wooden Horse trio escaped

Items used by an RAF officer to break out of a German prisoner-of-war camp in the famous Wooden Horse escape will go on display for the first time.

The objects, including his civilian disguise, a homemade compass, magnetised razor blades and a locket will go on show at London's Imperial War Museum as part of the Great Escapes exhibition.

They belonged to Oliver Philpot, who was one of three men to escape from Stalag Luft III in 1943.

With Michael Codner and Eric Williams, he dug his way out of the camp hidden by a wooden vaulting horse. While fellow prisoners exercised, beneath the horse the three men dug a tunnel just 18in square and 100ft long.

Once outside, the men adopted disguises and managed to travel to safety in Sweden.

Their exploits formed the basis of the 1950 film the Wooden Horse.

Michael Codner, Eric Williams and Ollie Philpot in Sweden

Roger continued to write letters, this one to Nic one of his favourite nieces.

Kriegsgefangenenlager
Datum
22nd Oct 43.

Dear Nic. Whenever this arrives it is to wish you one & all a merry Christmas & I hope you get lots of good things and perhaps a little 'Pig-cheer' from Cleatham: how I shall be thinking of you all – I'm afraid we cant quite be home by then but lets hope it wont be so very long after. I keep myself busy – just finished making a clock which keeps good time inspite of a very loud tick: it is driven by a lump of concrete hung on boot laces. My next effort will be a boat for Michael & then it will be time for Home I hope.

My love to you and everyone.
Uncle Roger

The winter set in hard and cold with much snow. Red Cross parcels were eagerly awaited and shared out giving the duty cooks in each room a bit more scope with the tins of corned beef and spam, milk, jam, raisins and other goodies.

The camp by now had expanded north with a big, new, even more escape proof compound of huts on stilts housing a lot of Americans and Roger Bushell, the mining engineer known as Big X who was head of the escape committee. They decided to start three tunnels named Tom, Dick and Harry as no-one must mention tunnel, digging or escape. The committee decided to make one big breakout of a great many men, so the 'travel agents' Dean and Dawson set to work compiling maps and documents and travel permits, using the study areas of 'students' studying for exams as cover. The tailors set to work on civilian clothes, German uniforms, any adaption of RAF issue clothing to fit the escapers new identity. German lessons were very well attended, and only the slightest whiff of this secrecy blew across the North Compound to Roger and his friends, something about a 'big job brewing'. Later they heard one of the ways photos were made for the passports. German guards were bribed with cigarettes and chocolate to produce an old Leica camera, film and printing paper. James Hill took photos of the forty hopeful escapees. He arranged a fake séance with gloomy music on the gramophone, a pretend Ouija board surrounded by several RAF officers with blankets over their heads. Yellow cellophane from a biscuit box covered the light bulb and he was able to start developing and printing under one of the bunks. Interrupted by a knock at the door, two German officers stood there. He moved the Ouija board pointer and called "Marshall Foch, are you there, when is the war going to end?" The German officers glanced round the room and left shaking their heads in disbelief, leaving James and his assistant to continue their work.

Christmas came with some Red Cross parcels getting through, rations were very tight now. The prisoners in Stalag Luft III were hungry most of the time, and the hunger spread throughout Germany and across Europe. Diversions from the theatre pantomime, and the orchestra helped, the church was regularly packed too. With so little food most men made use of the library, just walking the circuit once or twice a day with friends in the biting wind. The guards would provide information and almost anything for some home brewed alcohol, coffee, chocolate, or a few minutes warmth in a hut. 1944 did not start well for Roger whose letters contained the bad news of his father's death and later on in the summer when her roses were in bloom, his mother fell in the garden. Skipworth found her, she died soon after and was laid to rest beside his father on the south side of the church at Manton. He later received an unexpected letter from Mr Middleton one of the Cleatham workers who wrote to him to say he had been to his father and mother's funerals and that poor old Emma was well.

On the night of 24th of March a single shot was heard, and later bursts of machine gun fire from the North Compound towers. Roger and his mess suspected the 'Big Job' had been discovered. Hundreds of miles away in England, Joshey was screaming in the terror of a nightmare, a man standing over her bed ready to kill her if she showed she was awake, and a steady string of men crawling out from under her bed in a line, and through the door, desperation in their awkward speed.

As the days went by several escapers were returned to the camp and put in the 'cooler' for two weeks of isolation, unrelenting cold and very poor rations, soup – mainly potatoes and water with some Reich bread. Then Roger heard the terrible news. The Kommandant, Von Lindeiner was arrested and taken away, replaced by Oberst Braune who called the Senior British Officer, Group Captain Massey to his office. "Forty one of your officers have been shot trying to evade capture". "How many were wounded?" "None. I cannot give you any more information." Everyone was stunned – they knew it was murder. For days the Luftwaffe guards told the prisoners 'you must not blame the Luftwaffe – it was the Gestapo'. They later discovered Hitler had given a direct order to shoot all the 73 men who escaped but some of his senior officers refused. Other names were added to the list of dead until there were 50 including Roger Bushell. Everyone in the camp knew someone who had been shot.

Details of the planned 200 man escape filtered through, the three big tunnels, the many dummy tunnels, incredible depths, tunnel 'Tom' found when outside the wire and destroyed. Finally tunnel 'Harry' in Hut 104 was re-opened and completed. It had a 'railway' for transporting sand and eventually escapers, and an air conditioning system made from a kit bag and some bellows, even electric light which ran off the camp lighting system.

Eventually the prisoners were allowed to build a memorial for their friends in a local cemetery. Designed by Squadron Leader Hartnell-Beavis, a former architect, and built by a working party of officers under parole with an armed escort. The urns containing the ashes of the 50 were buried there.

The Great Escapers' memorial

With spring came better news of the war, Stalingrad fell in May and the Eastern front was cracking up, the Russians advancing. The Allies great Normandy landings started in June, illicit radios crackling with news, surely Roger thought we shall be home soon. Speculation was high, would the Russians release us or would the Allies arrive first. Sports were resumed, a long distance relay race meant a lot of men keeping fit pounding round the circuit.

Minor tensions in the six-men rooms were usually solved by a man moving to another room, but Roger had a problem room. Four of the men played cards constantly and when the other two needed the table for preparing supper or playing chess war broke out, so he took a square of plywood, tacked on thin strips of wood to make edges, added string, pulleys and a counter balance weight so the 'card table' could be elevated, with cards laid out if necessary at a moment's notice and secured to a hook in the wall. A temporary peace ensued.

German notices everywhere declared 'Escaping is no longer a sport. You will be shot.' So energies had to be channelled in another direction, the tailors repaired the shabby worn clothes as best they could in case of another bad winter here. The tunnellers had just one left from under seat 13 in the theatre. It was aimed at the hut where the Germans kept their rifles so the prisoners could arm themselves if the local starving population overran the camp, or as was rumoured Hitler used them as hostages.

Roger's thoughts turned to home and with Janett's encouraging letters he began to plan for life after the War, writing a letter to the Agricultural Advice Service.

Letter to Mr Henderson
Agricultural Advice Service
(Written after three years in a P.O.W. Camp)

Having read 'The Farming Ladder' together with article on your methods, in the Farmer and Stockbreeder with considerable interest, I should be grateful if you would care to hear the views of one who is a Serviceman for the time being, and happens to be a member of that most highly criticised members of the Community (and rightly so) the son of a 'Gentleman Farmer'.

I feel it is necessary in view of what it allows to say a brief word about my circumstances. My Father was a North Lincolnshire Farmer and I spent my first five years after leaving school on his farm: at the end of this period my elder brother came home and this together with the depression made me decide to fend for myself for a while at least, so I went into the Air Force. I fully intended to return to the land after five years, but, with the gathering War Clouds I decided – rightly or wrongly to remain in the Service.

Now after 3 years of captivity my Parents have died and left me certain interests in the land. I cannot state my feelings too deeply towards my responsibilities, except to say quite simply that this is a trust which I shall not evade no matter what the cost. I have therefore determined to leave no stone unturned to myself for the task in hand which I well know to be no light matter.

The first point in my plan is to spend at least a year or more – probably two learning 'The New Farming'.

My purpose in writing is therefore to ask whether you intend to continue your policy of training pupils and if so would you be prepared to consider an application from me shortly after the cessation of hostilities. I fully realize the import of this.

Yours sincerely,
Roger H Maw

During his time in the camp Roger had always kept his interest in farming having lively conversations with the men who had imaginary farms. They had maps of the land, drawings of the buildings, planned their work every day, ploughing, haymaking, lambing and so on. Their 'escape' was their farm, Roger's was his woodwork and inventions; spending time in the 'cooler' for minor infringement of the German regulations – even there he would walk the wrong way round the tiny exercise yard declaring it to be his right under the Geneva Convention!

Autumn came, the onset of another bitter winter, all the prisoners on just German food now - sour black bread, sausages of congealed blood, mouldy potatoes, thin barley or pea soup and cheese with a disgusting taste. The prisoners thought the guards fared no better, and the Russian workers worse.

The Red Cross were having difficulties threading their way across war torn Europe with its craters in the roads, blown up bridges, and overcrowded railways. The theatre crew continued work to produce yet another splendid pantomime. The men really looked forward to an evening at the theatre, polishing buttons and shoes. Tickets were by allocation as the theatre was not big enough for them all at once. Tom increasingly busy practising his violin for the orchestra's performance of Handel's Messiah with a choir of 80 which was memorable. The huts were decorated with tin stars cut from cans. When mail did get through it was eagerly received. Just before Christmas the Red Cross parcels arrived, with tinned turkey and plum pudding. Very few messes had saved up raisins to make a cake this year, and most of the stills had run dry. Church in the theatre was so well attended it was overflowing with ragged men, blankets over their heads against the bitter cold.

At this time, January 1945, strong rumours spread through the camp of a planned mass evacuation to march the prisoners away from the advancing Russians, possibly to hold them hostage in return for their own German prisoners. So men began packing their most treasured and useful possessions. The Canadians made backpacks with a wooden framework which converted to a sledge. More Red Cross parcels arrived from Lubeck and the senior officers decided to release them straight away, having been on poor rations since September the prisoners needed strengthening for whatever lay ahead, and encouraging to keep fit pounding round the perimeter track in the sub zero temperatures.

January 27th more news came through of the Russian advance speeded up considerably by American transport, so plans for evacuations redoubled, sledges built, rucksacks fashioned from kit bags, endless sorting of clothes and possessions, stoves glowed with wood torn from beds and walls. Roger packed his most precious letter and photographs, his diaries and details of the clock inside his shirt. Then he put on layers of clothes, everything he possessed, and in the improvised backpack some Red Cross parcel rations and the precious clock.

The prisoners were told to eat all they could as a huge pile of Red Cross parcels would be free to all as they left the camp. Great blocks of escapers 'dog food' were quickly mixed and divided, condensed milk, chocolate, porridge oats and Bemax, easy to carry and a little gives a lot of energy.

Roger and his mess huddled round the stove, "Shut the door", someone yelled. "I would but the Canadians took it to make another sledge."

Heavy snow was falling, the daylight fading when guards rushed from hut to hut shouting 'Rous Rous you leave in one hour'. By midnight there were bonfires burning outside, prisoners walking freely between the huts to visit friends, and search for better footwear among the discarded piles of clothes, the Goons plans were in chaos and by 2 a.m. they decided the East Compound would leave at 6 a.m. Very few beds had survived so men lay where they could, nearer the stoves on piles of surplus clothes. By now they had chosen their travelling companions mostly twos and threes, some loners, some teams of four or six with one big sledge to haul between them.

The Goons planned 6 a.m. start was delayed by men making tea and eating as much as their aching stomachs would allow for breakfast. Then slowly struggling through the snow - 10°C into the German compound. Queueing for the Red Cross parcels was a scene beyond imagination for the ever hungry prisoners, they could take as much as they could carry. Some tinned food was lobbed over the wire into the skeletal Russian prisoners compound. Then slowly they straggled to the open gate, Roger murmured the prayer he had used on every take off 'Please God' and they were off.

THE GREAT MIGRATION

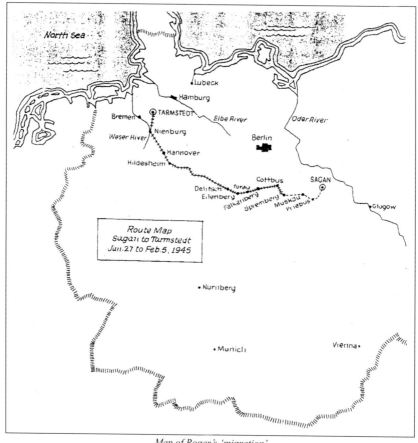

Map of Roger's 'migration'

Shuffling through the open gates in the early morning snow light, with all the food they could carry, seemed like a dream, there was a sense of freedom, almost adventure. The wind was biting cold, beards and moustaches froze in the sub zero temperatures. Roger soon found the icy cold creeping into his boots and mitts, his sledge with its Klim tin covered runners ran well at first, and he strode out to try and keep up with the younger men. As Roger's hut was one of the last to leave there were frequent hold ups ahead with sledges overturning, or men too exhausted to continue lying in the snow to rest. Roger used short stops to nibble on 'escapers' cake or a few raisins. Longer stops he could fire up his home made Tommy's cooker, a sort of firebox within a tin which ran on wisps of paper and tiny scraps of wood which he kept dry in his pocket. Unhooking his tin mug from his belt he could melt snow to make dried soup or coffee, which often froze before he could finish it. He checked his little homemade compass, they were travelling roughly South West away from the advancing Russians. Roger was surprised to find they were not the only ones on the road, crowds of refugees pushing prams and carts full of household goods and children. The prisoners stopped to help one family get their horse out of a snowdrift. As the packs and sledges seemed to get heavier men threw things out, and shadowy figures rushed from the sheltering pines to retrieve them. Then the blizzard started again but Roger could occasionally hear the muffled drone of planes overhead. The Senior British Officer (SBO) had issued an order before they left, no escaping, in these icy conditions and allied troops could be anywhere, the ragged muffled prisoners could not easily be identified.

The column eventually struggled into Halbau, 16 kilometres from Sagan. A demand from the SBO sent the exhausted Goons to find accommodation for the night. During the icy wait darkness fell and the locals came out to barter. Roger got some eggs and potatoes in exchange for soap and coffee. After an hour or so they moved up to the market place but it was crammed with refugees. By now Roger's pack was too heavy. He saw a door with a brass plate like a doctors, knocked on it, and gave the surprised lady his precious clock. Eventually billets were found in schools, halls, farmyards and the propeller works. Roger cooked his potatoes and eggs and fell asleep.

The next day's march seemed harder, the sledges heavier, men now suffering from chilblains and those with poor shoes the onset of frostbite.

It was bleak, open country with 10,000 men on the road. Roger thought briefly of Tom Wilson left behind in the camp hospital.

In a haze of exhaustion they reached Freiwaldau only to find no room there, with temperatures dropping to -20∞C they moved on to the village of Lieppa where Roger and fellow prisoners packed into the ancient church, no heating but there was light and they soon settled in. It was a bizarre scene with socks drying over light bulbs on chandeliers. Roger hung his clothes to dry on the organ pipes thinking briefly how shocked the people of Kirton church would be! Someone had a record player and Glenn Miller blared out cheerfully. The font was bubbling away with a big stew. Card players fell asleep suddenly in mid deal, the result of intense cold. Some men were cooking over open fires outside, while a BBC voice from a secret radio announced the heavy bombing of German cities.

The Padre looked up old church records and found it to be a Lutheran church dating back to 1806 and thought it could have been used to house exhausted French soldiers in their retreat from Moscow. Roger curled up and slept fitfully with perhaps as many as one thousand RAF men from all over the world.

The weather turned slightly warmer and the snow turned to slush – some of the more skilled sledge pullers had made wheels, the Canadians lightened their loads and pulled their sledges up as backpacks padded by spare clothes.

February 1st and Roger and his friends prepared for the 28 kilometres night march to Spremberg to go by rail to the Bremen area. No frost tonight, delays as Goons attempted to count prisoners in the dark. Locals had warned of the annual thaw coming early. Just before midnight the column moved off through the slush up the cobbled hill into open country. Roger saw some abandoned sledges but most people struggled on in the bright moonlight, stopping briefly to nibble 'escaper cake'. The roadsides were littered with clothes and food abandoned from the collapsing sledges. The confusion of exhaustion made it so difficult to decide what to leave by the road and what to keep. Finally at dawn they fell into a hay barn and slept or passed out.

Roger woke mid morning, people packing to move out. The Goons said only a few more kilometres to Spremberg but it seemed a long way with diarrhoea and bad feet.

At last the prisoners reached Spremberg, the ragged column turned into the 8th Panzer division's reserve depot where there seemed to be some sort of organization, uniformed soldiers issued hot barley soup and a bread ration, leaving the prisoners to sit on the warm dry concrete floor and sort out their packs before marching to the trains.

The old Luftwaffe guards emerged from the depot sickbay, patched up to escort the Kriegies for the next leg of the journey. They marched the last few kilometres in the dark arriving at 1700 hours to find the waiting train was all cattle trucks. The Senior British Officer's protests were to no avail, there was nothing else, but during the wait some USA Red Cross parcels were issued. Promises were made to the Senior British Officer of regular halts for natural functions and drinks of water, and the prisoners were crammed in at least sixty to a truck filthy from the previous occupants both two and four legged.

Roger supplied a few nails to knock into the walls to hang backpacks. Fat lamps from Goon margarine were lit, chinks in truck walls enlarged to check on the route, and essential chinks in the floor for 'natural functions'. It was ages before the train moved off and the air was foul. After three hours they were let out briefly to stretch and relieve themselves, then the bolts were slammed shut and the train coughed slowly off into the darkness.

Planes droned overhead, Roger prayed they would not bomb this train. The night's journey was erratic with shunting and stops, one where they were let out briefly to squat beside the track, find a big can for a urinal and scrounge some hot water from a railway worker. The train seemed to go North, then West through Wilden, crossing the river Elbe at Torgan, then Eilenburg. The air in the truck was appalling, men with diarrhoea and vomiting made everyone feel queasy, so being a lookout near the crack by the door was a welcome duty. Roger dozed at times cramped on the filthy floor, proper sleep was impossible, he heard bombs exploding near the larger cities, and was roused by the occasional sing song.

Conditions worsened during the second night, locked in for 12 hours with no water was a nightmare. The lookout announced Magdeburg Brunswick and Hildesheim, air raid sirens were heard. At last day break and the doors slid back in Hanover, a bucket of water handed in – doors shut again but opened a hundred yards down the track and men tumbled out to relieve themselves in full view of the shocked Hanoverians! The short pause meant time to try and clean out the truck a bit, and eat something from the Red Cross parcels. Eventually after two days and nights the train stopped at Tarnstedt Ost and the weary Kriegies struggled out in the heavy rain. Roger heard their destination was Marlag und Milag Nord, an old Naval camp, surely not barbed wire again. Slowly they shouldered their packs and set off the last three kilometres along a muddy track, then a long wait outside the camp gates as the Luftwaffe guards handed over to the Marines running the camp.

The long straggling line of prisoners covered in the filth of the cattle trucks were now encased in a layer of mud, but rumours of hot showers and food filtered down the line as they sat waiting to get into the camp. Ten men to a hut, taken in out of the rain and strip-searched from their horrible clothing, camp heating kaput so the fantasy of hot showers receded into the darkness as Roger fell onto an old straw mattress beneath a leaking roof and passed out leaving the rats to continue their journeys to and fro uninterrupted.

February 5th. The camp looked even worse in daylight, broken windows and stoves, damp uneven smelly brick floors, roofs leaking and rat droppings amid the piles of rubbish. There was one cold shower working in the open which Roger found good to freshen up. He was once more in charge of a hut, number 21, with a lot of men from his hut in Sagan. He formed a working party of the few fit men to clean up the place and patch the roof as best they could. Most stoves were broken so they got all the little tin can Tommy cookers they could to brew up hot drinks for the weaker men. Red Cross parcels began to come in, and there was a lot of black market bargaining with some Goons through the wire in the next compound. A pit was dug beneath a stove in a small room near the cookhouse where a radio was installed, and on February 14th the news of raids on Dresden with 25,000 dead was greeted in silence, the firestorm, and so many refugees.

The regular appells were not well attended at first as too many men were unfit to stand in the cold wind, but with more food coming in most of them rallied and started working to become fit again as rumour had it there would be another march.

Working parties on parole with guards were allowed outside the camp to collect wood. It was hard work for unfit men but some extra rations were supplied for the working party and it was good to be outside the wire and hear bird song between the steady drone of aircraft. So camp life resumed its normal pattern of appells and sport, reading and playing cards.

March 25th the Germans allowed the prisoners to hold a memorial service for their 50 murdered comrades from the Great Escape one year previously. They stood in rows on the parade ground, heads bared in the spring sunshine, larks singing overhead joining 'O God our help in ages past'. The names were read out one by one. The Padre said a prayer followed by The Last Post and Reveille on a battered trumpet – then a minute's silence.

Towards the end of March the 'kitchen radio' announced the Allies had reached Bremen, east of Tarmstedt. April 6th an air raid but no damage to the camp, a lot of air activity and rumours of another march, so urgent preparations produced carts and huge cooked meals, stoves fuelled from the wooden hut walls. Messages scribbled on remaining ones to allied troops to let our people know we are safe so far, and a large sign RAF POW with a big arrow pointing North left on the parade ground.

Eventually the column moved off North, walking slowly, resting at will, the Goons had brought horses and carts to speed up the proceedings, so some of the weaker men could ride for a while. Roger enjoyed the spring sunshine, the guards were no trouble, but suddenly an allied plane drove at them spewing bullets, everyone dived for the ditches. There were some deaths and the injured were left in a local hospital.

Nights were spent in open fields which they clearly marked POW in straw in the middle. Groups of men made fires, collected straw and built shelters by the hedges, others bartered for eggs, kinder wagons (prams), potatoes and chickens. Several wheelbarrows went missing and as the journey progressed towards the Elbe river most men walked free of backpacks, even carrying some of the guards packs. Blossom came out on the fruit trees and men washed in rivers or streams, washing clothes which they hung to dry on hedges. There was no shortage of food but Roger felt queasy at times with the odd diet. Farming aircrew would occasionally nip into a barn and milk a cow so diets improved. Rumours of allied progress abounded and heavy bombing was heard near Hamburg. Crossing the Elbe was a risky business with Allied planes shooting up boats, so a short church service accompanied by bird song was held on the river bank the night before the crossing.

Delays next morning meant that clouds rolled in by midday making the crossing safer from aircraft fire. Two old ferry boats worked tirelessly on their fifteen minute journeys, and in four hours the long ragged column, complete with prams and barrows was across safely. Roger had seen the docks and submarine pens upstream towards Hamburg and could understand the RAF's constant watch on the Elbe. Sunny days walking, fairly comfortable nights in fields, and enough food so Roger enjoyed looking at the farming in this pleasant part of Germany. Rumours about their destination and the end of the war were constantly discussed. Rainy days the journey seemed endless and the cold damp nights. Roger saw and heard a lot of aircraft and noise but noticeably less Luftwaffe although it was rumoured the new jet fighters were using the autobahn for a runway as they had so few aerodromes left.

Eventually the weary column turned into a huge farmyard Trenthorst, part of a very large modern farming estate, big modern buildings, pedigree cattle and roomy haylofts with a nearby lake for washing, fishing and laundry. Next morning Roger heard big vehicles and was amazed to see nine trucks loaded with Red Cross parcels. The Senior British Officer warned everyone to stay put to be liberated safely.

May 2nd at noon a single Bren gun carrier drove into the courtyard to announce their LIBERATION – such scenes of unrestricted joy, 1,500 airforce officers no longer prisoners.

At a special Camp Parade, Lieutenant Colonel Coomb outlined the plans for their homeward journey ending with 'Patience and please don't cause trouble'. There were three cheers for the King and for the Senior British Officer, a cheery Canadian who had done such a great job in negotiating with the Goons. Life developed into one big party and Roger 'hitched a ride' on an American bomber, his last war time flight.

—— DREAM FULFILLED ——

I only remember my mother crying once, and that was long after Father's return from the prison camp. It was her optimism and cheerfulness throughout his captivity that caused Joss and I to be certain of his return. I must admit being slightly scared of this event.

As a little boy of four my only memory of him was in photographs. We lived in Bournemouth, Mother, my sister Joss and I together with mother's mother and Aunty Maudy. The occasional bomb would land as the Germans targeted Southampton, and offloaded any bombs they had left. So I remember the windows being taped, and the 'Morrison' bed. A massive construction of steel girders in the dining room. We all climbed into it when the sirens went, secure in the knowledge that even if the house was hit we would be safe from falling rubble. It never happened, but to a small boy it was an adventure.

I was often reminded of Father at meal times when Mother surrounded a tasty morsel of meat with vegetables. The game was to eat all the vegetables (the Germans) so that Father (the tasty morsel) could escape and come home. So I suppose I was on high alert when the event happened. I remember lying awake on the night he returned, feeling slightly scared now that the photographs would turn into a real person. A car door slammed, joyful voices were raised, then all went quiet as I drifted off to sleep.

Morning came and Mother took me into her bedroom to see Daddy. I'm sure Joss was there, but I was only aware of the photo in the bed. I have a vivid memory of crinkly hair, a big moustache and a hand appearing from the bedclothes, holding a fascinating toy crane. The ice being truly broken, I got on with my childhood. Unbeknown to us, Mother had written countless letters to Father while he was in the prison camp, and all these were safely brought back having survived the long march at the end of hostilities. My dearest mother had kept alive their hopes and dreams in these letters which, I am sure was a major factor in Father adapting to civilian life after some 20 years in the Air Force.

The Hillman 10 was started up after its lonely vigil in the garage. My mother remembers hearing my voice from the back seat of the car, long before Father's return.

"You nasty Germans, I'll smack your bottoms!" I do not remember this remark, but I recall the smell of leather and petrol during my many imaginary adventures whilst seated in the vehicle. On special occasions we would go on short trips for family picnics, with Father at the wheel.

The picnic

I recall the day we moved house. With the car and trailer loaded up, we set off for the very short journey to our new home. I'm sure my granny and her sister welcomed our departure. A large, heavy folding screen had been placed on top of the trailer. Presumably, my Father thought the weight of it would keep it there without a rope. I have a vivid memory, as I looked back, of the draught screen flying off the trailer like a giant Neolithic bird, and my Father uttering words I had never heard before – could they have been in German?

My Father's first venture into commerce was that of a toymaker. He was brilliant with tin and wood. Unfortunately, the man whom he went into partnership with ran off with some of Father's savings, and this terminated the venture. I have a vivid memory of an extraordinary model submarine that he constructed. He took me along for the 'test drive' in a local swimming pool. We were the only people there so I assume Father had special permission to use the facilities.

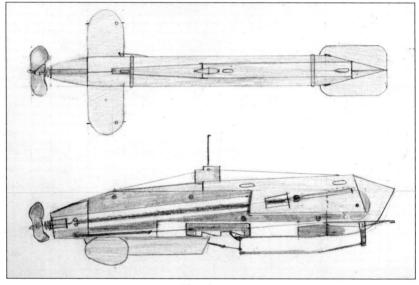

The submarine

The submarine was elastic powered, and once fully wound up using the propeller, this amazing craft set off on the surface of the crystal clear water. In less than two yards it dived and went to the bottom of the pool, where it levelled out. The elastic ran out and the submarine rose to the surface. I know the design had evidently been worked on in theory during my Father's time in Stalag Luft III. Father was once asked what his role in the camp was, the answer; "Twofold, one to keep up the morale of the men in my hut and two to annoy the guards as much as possible". To understand his reply, one must bear in mind that Father was much older than the average prisoner. Also, being a Wing Commander with his long flying record and public school background he was well-suited for the task.

While in Stalag III Father had written a letter to the ADAS (Agricultural Development and Advisory Service) concerning a re training programme, prior to searching for farm land in his beloved Lincolnshire. We don't know if a reply was forthcoming. However, the opportunity arose for him to work on a large mixed arable farm in neighbouring Dorset. It is worth noting that Father had been away from the land for 20 years. Technology in the world of the RAF had moved from the bi-plane with open cockpits in the late 1920s to the jet planes used by the Germans in the closing weeks of the war. Technology in farming, in contrast, grew at a snail's pace, due to the Great War 1914-1918 and the recent conflict. Government money was scarce so the machines used in agriculture had changed little since Father was helping out at Cleatham. Tractors had been used frugally prior to the war years and the horse was still much in demand. In 1939 on British farms there were 20 horses to every tractor. As the need for food production grew, so did the need for mechanization.

Many farmers supplemented their existing 'horse' power with a tractor, this meant adapting tired out of date machinery. The government demanded that thousands of grass land acreage should be put into food production, hundreds of those acres needed draining. This was a formidable job for farmers which they willingly undertook, with extra labour drafted in - the Land Army. There would be changes in the coming years as cutbacks were eased. I still have my food rationing book which declares rationing was not terminated till 1953.

Father returned from Germany at the cessation of the war in May 1945. Within seven months he was offered an opportunity to be trained in modern farming methods on the farm of Richard Trehane, later to become Sir Richard, knighted for his contributions to agriculture in 1968. Richard was the ideal mentor for my Father. Born in 1913, youngest son of James Trehane, and member of the Milk Marketing Board, Richard was educated at Monkton Coomb, after which he read Agriculture at Reading University. Reading his obituary (December 22nd 2001) his first love was the long established Friesian herd at the family farm, but his love of all things agricultural came a close second, and so it was that in the

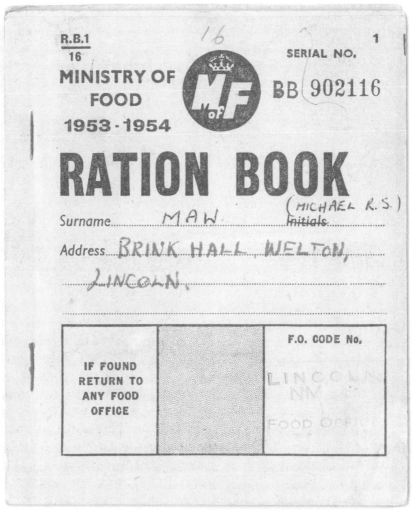

February of 1946 Father signed up for a year on Richard's mixed farm at Hampreston. The location of the farm was some 30 miles from our home in Boscombe, Bournemouth. By this time Father had acquired a 250 cc BSA motorbike which would transport him in an hour to Hampreston, where he would set off at dawn and return each evening.

1946 was a special year for the family as on August 20th our little sister Tessa was born.

Joss, Tessy and Mike

By Christmas of 1946, Father's time at Hampreston was over and he joined with his family to celebrate and contemplate the coming year with the search for a farm in Lincolnshire. On the morning of January 24th we all awoke to find a generous covering of snow. This preceded the worst winter of the century. The cold was intense and the snow relentless, with ten foot drifts and the mighty Thames frozen over. It was recorded that snow fell every day until March 16th. Lincolnshire, the promised land, was one of many counties completely cut off. Eventually the thaw came and with it floodwaters. Some 31 counties were affected. The long awaited summer of 1947 was gloriously hot. So Father, in the late spring of 1947 returned full of enthusiasm to Lincolnshire to begin the search so that his ambition (held for twenty years) might be fulfilled.

At this point in time my Father's family home at Cleatham was owned by his older brother Dick. This had come about due to the death of both their parents during the war years. The estate was of some size: two farms, Cleatham and the Low Farm, both managed by Dick, and a further acreage St Helena, which had been left to my Father in trust, some 180 acres of medium loam. The farm was managed by a tenant Mr Warwick and the tenancy could only be terminated when the incumbent retired, some 13 years into the future.

St Helena

Father's search for a suitable farm was rewarded in September 1947. I was told at farming college, that the place to start searching for land sales was in a local hostelry, and I am sure this information was relevant in Father's case. The area of the search was a 25 mile radius of Cleatham. Father knew the land in that area, and so it was an obvious place to start. Brink Hall Farm at Welton Cliff, 15 miles from Lincoln, was 200 acres, 40 acres being 'cliff land', and moderately stoney. The rest was medium loam, badly in need of drainage, but in good heart. The owner was retiring in March 1948 and was happy to arrange a private sale. This included the farmhouse; a splendid solid construction of limestone and two cottages. A price of £70 an acre was agreed and in March of that year a mortgage of £14,000 was taken out to finance the long dream.

My sister remembers:-

I remember so clearly the excitement of exploring our new home, the smell of damp whitewash in the cellar with its dark secret passage to the hall. The little curved passage half way up the front stairs to my bedroom, Mike and I rushing out into the farmyard to see a small haystack apparently on fire making its way steadily towards the cow shed. It turned out to be Mr Coultan our cowman/gathy smoking his pipe while carrying hay to the cows.

Brink Hall

Brink Hall Farm. Feeding the chickens

Another memory of a cold winter night and Dad cutting a lot of bread into small squares to put in a battered enamel dish full of milk, and setting it on the kitchen stove to warm before carrying it out into the snow for the yard cats.

Two large gas cylinders near the larder provided light in every room, boosted by paraffin lamps. The gas light was poor and a vivid memory of mother darning socks with a battery powered 'mushroom' comes to mind.

The Morris Oxford

The trusty Morris Oxford would be hitched to the caravan and we would set out for Kelling Heath in Norfolk. Ours was no ordinary caravan. Let me explain. The van was some seventeen foot long, the back panel was sloping and accommodated two French doors (great for accessibility) and made sure that the doors were self closing. Because there were four berths and six in the family (including our foster brother Doug) Father decided to build an extension to the caravan, making the total length on site some twenty four foot! The hinge pins in the French doors were replaced with quick release pins – the doors removed and set on one side. Two side plywood panels, each with a light frame and a window were butted up to the rear of the caravan and securely fixed to brackets. The back panel (a mirror image of the sloping rear of the caravan) was designed and when fixed to the side panels it accommodated the French windows. These were secured to their hinges by the same quick release pins. One important feature of the rear of the caravan roof was that it projected several inches over the rear panel, so that when the extension was fitted the ridge pole (which supported the tarpaulin) made a weather tight joint allowing the rainwater to drip from the caravan roof onto the (new) extension roof. A row of hooks at the top of the side sections held the tarpaulin in place. As a bonus Father constructed a plywood and tarpaulin tent for the Elsan (chemical toilet).

Holidays were taken during the two weeks before harvest.

All panels including the tarpaulin were stored in the caravan. The rear panel was in two sections to fit through the French window aperture and the doors were replaced and locked.

The only downside to this extraordinary camping phenomena was the extra weight the new extension added when towing. The Morris Oxford was underpowered normally, and did well to haul the caravan all those miles to Kelling. I remember following behind in the Wolseley and watching the caravan sway alarmingly at speed of over 40 mph.

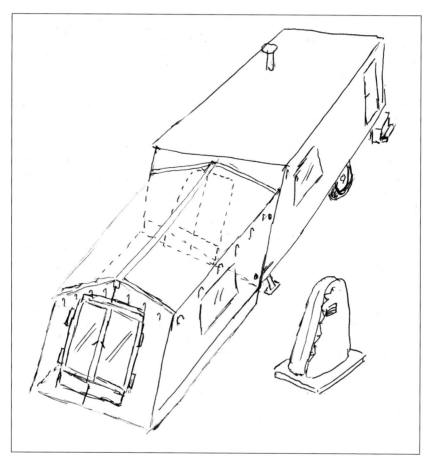

After several enjoyable summers at Kelling, the caravan (without the extension) was sited permanently in the wooded area of the campsite. We shall never forget the ingenuity of this construction. Another way my Dad had of expressing his love for the family.

I remember well an occasion when, after a nasty fall which resulted in a broken humerus, I finished up in hospital flat on my back. My left arm was suspended vertically from a pin through the elbow, and my upper arm was encased in plaster. This position was to last for eight weeks. Normal life was suspended, even reading was almost impossible. As an active teenager I found this unbearable, but my dear dad with his logical mind came up with an idea that brought me great relief and transformed my day. The idea was a reading table, clamped cunningly to the right hand side of the bed. He had measured and drawn out the 'reader', and returned with it. It fitted perfectly, the angle could be adjusted with one hand and as a master stroke of genius he had fitted a boiled egg holder.

Needless to say the NHS (National Health Service) were not impressed, but by the time they protested I had been using it for half a day (they had to admit eventually that it was improving the quality of my horizontal existence). Six years prior to this I contracted double pneumonia and was sent to a special hospital outside Lincoln. On visiting days Dad would bring his carpentry tools and mother and I would watch him making a village for my Dinky toys (a roadway and several houses).

About this time a letter arrived from the Air Ministry (Overleaf)

Two horses were inherited with the farm as well as a trusty petrol paraffin Fordson Major tractor. I think we may have eventually had two tractors, one with 'spud wheels' (metal rims with knobs on to assist with ploughing) and the other with ordinary rubber tyres. It is said that people of a certain age recall summers being longer and hotter. This was certainly so. Harvesting in that era was done by a binder, pulled by a tractor. The binder was an ingenious contraption. A seven foot cutting bed cut the crop close to the ground. The crop was urged by a flail to fall onto an endless moving slatted canvas, which carried the crop into the mechanism that tied individual sheaves with a strong hairy string known as binderband or farmers' friend. These were then spat out in orderly lines, to be picked up by hand and joined with seven others to make stooks or stouks across the field. I recall my Father seated on the binder clutching a 12-bore shot gun ready to deal with the rabbits who, on occasion would burst out of the standing crop.

To complete a harvest (of 140 acres) we needed at least a month and a half of good weather. The giant Combines of today go in when the grain is very ripe and almost falling out of the husk. With a binder you went in while the grain was in the last stage of ripening so that, by the time the crop had been cut, stooked, loaded onto carts to be stacked in the yard, the grain had not shaken out, and was waiting for the threshing machine to come along in the winter. The dry grain then finished up in bags to be sold before Christmas.

TEL. HOLBORN 3434 Extn.

Correspondence on the subject of this
letter should be addressed to :—
THE UNDER SECRETARY OF STATE,
AIR MINISTRY
and should quote the reference :—
A.193704/54/O.A.R.

Your Ref.

AIR MINISTRY,

LONDON, W.C.2.

22nd June 1954

Sir,

    1.   I am commanded by the Air Council to inform you that,
in accordance with the provisions of the Navy, Army and Air Force
Reserves Act, 1954, you are no longer liable to recall to
service with the Royal Air Force, being over 45 years of age.
You will therefore be required to relinquish your commission in
the Royal Air Force.
Relinquishment takes effect from 10th February 1954,
and the requisite notification will appear in the London
Gazette in due course.

    2.   The Council have granted you permission to retain
the rank of Wing Commander.   . This grant of rank does
not confer the right to any emoluments, nor does it carry with
it permission to wear uniform save on the special occasions
mentioned in paragraph 214 of Queen's Regulations and Air
Council Instructions, a copy of which is enclosed.

    3.   The Air Council take this opportunity to convey to you
their warm thanks for the services you have rendered to the
Royal Air Force, which they greatly appreciate.

        I am, Sir,
           Your obedient Servant,

A E Slater

 Wing Commander R.H. MAW, DFC (32090)

After returning from boarding school I spent a year working with Father,
and then had a spell at farming college. My reflections working or
just being with my dad are patchy, so I will just highlight a number of
memories.

Firstly his mode of dress. He wore baggy tweed trousers, held up with
binder band (double knotted to avoid gravity taking over) and a very
battered leather jerkin topped off, in the summer, with a straw hat. This

Harvest home

seemed to be the mode of dress until his retirement in 1965. The winter dress (the quin set – five sweaters) was many layers covered by a forces great coat tied again with binder band. Binder band was the toughest string available at the time. Many things on the farm owed their life to binder band. I remember Father making rope out of it during the winter months.

Secondly, I remember clearly that Father was tone deaf, like his Uncle Harold. He admitted that like Uncle Harold he only knew two tunes, "One was God Save the King and the other wasn't". Nevertheless, while I was working with him he would often hum two or three bars of a certain tune. Even now twenty years after his death the melody will suddenly enter my thoughts, but it is impossible to intentionally recall it. I just have to wait until the very distinctive melody randomly appears in my brain, and it goes as swiftly as it came. This is an unexpected reminder of my dear Dad which lingers in my long term memory.

Thirdly, Father's prowess as a carpenter was legendary. It enabled him to construct the famous 'Wooden Horse', and subsequent substantial buildings during his farming days. These buildings were constructed out of telegraph poles, railway sleepers, plywood and tin sheeting, each made to outlast an average life span.

When Father had finished work on these, he would step back to admire a certain joint or aspect of the construction and make the comment, 'It fits where it touches'.

After a number of years harvesting with the binder, Father invested in a Claas trailer Combine, which meant that all the corn was now in bags (1 cwt – 8 stone). The downside of this method of harvesting was that corn had to be sold immediately, and had to be harvested with a very low moisture content. This often meant turning the bags in the field to let them dry. All the bags had to be fetched into the yard and stored, and then sold at the current price, as soon as possible.

Interestingly the 1947 Agriculture Act laid the foundation for post war farm policy in the UK, establishing guaranteed prices for most farm products and deficiency payments. These made up the difference between the guaranteed price and the market price paid by the Exchequer, thus preserving the access to domestic markets for foreign supplies at world prices, and maintaining food prices to consumers at world levels.

Guaranteed prices were set annually. For a farmer on a low or no budget this was a Godsend.

During Father's time with Richard Trehane, he had not shared Richard's love of dairy cows, but learned a great deal about the arable side of farming, as well as growing grass for seed. Remember that Richard was chairman on the board of the UK Grassland Institute. The crops grown at Brink Hall were potatoes (20 acres), sugar beet (20 acres), grass for seed and oilseed rape (much later well before he retired). The rest of the acreage was used for wheat and barley.

It was inevitable, with the increase in technology that the way forward for growing cereals had to be the construction of a corn drier. This would simply mean that grain could be harvested with a higher moisture content, dried and stored to be sold after Christmas at an agreed price. Father went into overdrive, and with the help of the Agricultural Advisory experts put pencil to paper and began to plan and later construct the first 'in bin' installation in the area. The five 30 ton concrete bins were assembled by a local firm. All the conveyors and elevators, to move grain from one bin to another, were bought secondhand from Dukeries flour mill, reassembled and put to work. All the concrete work, the power house, and other facilities for dressing grain were done by Father and two employees. A mammoth task!

The drier really came into its own when the Claas trailer combine was replaced with a second hand Massey Harris self propelled combine. When the inboard tank was full of grain, the cereal was transferred by auger to a trailer – this operation could be done on the move. The trailer then tipped its load into the receiving pit – no more sacks, precious time saved. The whole operation done by two men.

The drier boasted the only safety system of its kind anywhere on the planet and yes, you've guessed it – binder band! Binder band ran over pulleys up into the roof and then ran back to the control panel which housed the three switches that controlled all the elevators and conveyors.

So, for example, if you fell off the gantry, you would be certain to fall past a long piece of binder band, grab it and pull. As you hit the ground there would be the satisfaction of knowing that, despite your injuries, all the elevators and conveyors would be switched off. Over the three electric switches there was a hinged construction of wood, having three corks. The construction was spring loaded with an elastic rope and when summoned by the binder band, it would crash down on the three switches, rendering the moving equipment immobile. People came from miles around to see the drier.

The 'pièce de la résistance' was the visit of the safety officer, who was so taken with this invention that, as he left, he walked past three items of machinery that had no guards or safety equipment of any kind.

Then there was the chicken alarm. Father bought 250 chickens and gave me the job of looking after them collecting and selling their eggs. A shed was adapted but it was soon apparent that the chickens needed a longer day to increase egg laying efficiency. Yes, there were time switches but they were expensive so Father decided to make one.

The following items were assembled, (and I wish I had kept the completed invention as a memorial to Father's unstoppable ingenuity). A biscuit tin, a few levers made from 20 gauge tin, a length of string, an alarm clock, a mouse trap and a pull switch. Picture the scene – chickens snoring. The alarm clock in the biscuit tin (securely fixed to a bracket) goes off. The key at the back of the clock rotates, the 20 gauge tin levers move as the string wraps itself round the key. The mouse trap is triggered, which in turn operates the pull switch, which turns on the lights, which wakes the chickens.

Father's eccentricity took on many forms. He was interviewed on several occasions, mainly about his involvement with the construction of the Wooden Horse. During an interview for television he announced to many thousands of viewers that one of the reasons that Germany lost two world wars was because they had no sense of humour!

Another occasion was during one of our visits to Smithfield Show, the main annual agricultural show in London. I remember a feeling of misgiving as we neared the Claas stand, and Father's eye fell upon an ingenious piece of equipment. A hay tedder that was hinged in several places for work on rough hillsides. It almost seemed as though the whole of Smithfield heard Father's statement, pronounced in a loud voice, "Trust the... Krauts to come up with something like this." From right behind us, the voice of a German salesman, "Can I help you sir?" I wanted to die. Strangely enough Father had, as mentioned, bought and used a German Claas trailer combine. Just in case Angela Merkel (Chancellor of Germany) is reading this, the engineering was without fault and the machine produced an excellent sample of grain.

By now (1960) Mr Warwick, the tenant at St Helena had retired, and I, having completed two years at farming college, moved in as manager. The farm was in desperate need of modernisation, and so it was that Father and I looked at the possibility of installing an 'on the floor' corn drier. This was basically a large shed with a central plywood air tunnel. Branching off from either side of the tunnel were small air tunnels, covered in hessian that ran under the corn. A three-phase electric fan blasted air through this system, and would dry corn with an 18% moisture content down to 15% at six foot high.

We went to various farm demonstrations to gather information about the project. It was on one of these occasions that Father and I were involved in a bizarre accident. The fact that neither of us was killed was a miracle. Our mode of transport for the day was an Austin Cambridge. This vehicle had for some weeks suffered from a 'flat spot' or lack of immediate acceleration. I had cured the fault by replacing the carburettor.

(Essential information) Our destination was Eastville near Boston in the Fens. The farm was situated just beyond an unmanned level crossing. The crossing gate, preventing access, was open all day. Having gathered much information about the project, I drove back to the crossing, slowed down and looked both ways. The line was clear and visibility was good. I cannot explain why, but I never saw the train. I heard the bellow of the horn and remember looking left past Father's head and seeing the buffer of the train some 20-25 yards away, closing at speed. My right foot pressed the accelerator to the floor, the new carburettor responded and the car (the bonnet was just over the first rail) leapt forward. The impact was level with the rear wheel. There were no seat belts as the law had not come into force. The car spun round, seemed to rotate in a clockwise direction, and came to rest upright and clear of the railway line. Father was no longer in the passenger seat. Shocked and confused I got out of the car, shouting "Dad! Dad!" I found him some yards away from the car, lying spread-eagled on a grassy bank. I had bitten through my lip during the accident, and as I knelt down beside my dear Dad, some of my blood landed on his head, and in my confusion I thought he must be dead – and then I heard the following statement, "This is very comfortable old boy." Our joy of being reunited was short-lived as the guard on the train came back to view the damage. An ambulance duly arrived and the hospital doctor could find no structural damage in me or my Father. As I reflect upon this incident, some 50 years ago now, I am convinced there is a God who intervenes in the affairs of men and through these waits for recognition (John 3, v. 16-17).

In 1962 Father had reached the age of 55 and mother had persuaded him to consider retiring at the age of 60. It is interesting to note that Father's life seemed to be in 20 year lots; his early life at Cleatham, his time in the RAF up to 1945, his farming life up to 1965 and then the subsequent 25 years of retirement. Now in 1963 there was this project of a grain store at St Helena. The 'in bin' drier which had been installed at Brink Hall several years before was being swiftly outmoded by bigger capacity combines which meant quicker ways of dealing with grain in bulk. So a 'dirty great shed' (Father's words) was designed, the cost of building it and installing an on-the-floor grain drier was worked out, and a government grant applied for. The shed was erected by a local firm. The central wind tunnel and air channels were constructed by Father with my help. The idea simply was to install a very powerful three-phase fan which blasted air down a central wind tunnel, bolted to the floor, with numerous wooden air channels teeing off from the central tunnel at floor level. Each channel was opened and closed (depending how much grain there was) by vertical slides operated from the top of the wind tunnel. Father was in seventh heaven. Marine ply and 3x2 timber were used in abundance.

The wind tunnel and channels were completed in a very short time, and were duly passed fit for purpose by the government. Father voiced the opinion that the wind tunnel was 'built like a brick privy' (reference to a well-made outside toilet of yester year). The final job was to construct some cheap grain walls to line the shed up to 7 foot high. This was simply and cheaply solved by acquiring some robust floor sections measuring 12 foot by 7 and assembled thus.

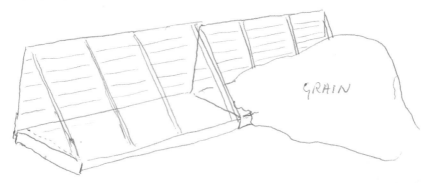

GRAIN

Once the grain was on the foot sections, flat iron supported the back sections (this was common practice), and the sections became immensely strong and immoveable. This was celebrated by the birth of my eldest daughter, Michaela in April of 1964, and the drier was put into use in the harvest of that year. For that year and the next we had to borrow the combine from Brink Hall, a distance of 30 miles from St Helena. This was driven over straight after finishing the harvest at Brink. It would be very easy to get bogged down with details of managing a grain store, but this is a story about my father and not a 'how to farm' manual. So I will finish this section with a funny but true agricultural story. Not about my father but something he appreciated enormously.

In the early days of the combine (it may well have been the Massey Harris combine) we had two men working at Brink Hall – Harry and Pete. Pete was the youngest and the main 'tractor' man. Harry was a solid hard working man, but was not into the present day technology. It was a harvest morning, bright and clear. The combine, having been greased, was ticking over in the yard. The seven foot bed was running, the flails slowly turning, and all the elevators were chattering. Harry and Pete were having a heated argument. Harry snatched Pete's well worn cloth cap that he was wearing, and threw it onto the slowly moving bed. From then on it was like a Laurel and Hardy film, Pete's cap disappeared into the bowels of the combine, to reappear minutes later, falling from the straw walkers at the rear of the machine, ruined, torn in several places. With a cry of rage, young Pete snatched Harry's soft felt trilby, and hurled it into the machinery, to be spat out minutes later, completely unscathed, not a mark on it! The mists of time have obscured what happened next, but I have the feeling that Father might have intervened diplomatically!

Back in March 1948, Father had taken out a mortgage (some £14,000) to purchase Brink Hall. This had finally been paid off, and so the plan of retirement began to take shape. St Helena farm (left in trust to Father from his father) was valued in 1965, and sold the following year. The money would be invested and serve a 100% mortgage on building a bungalow. The land having already been purchased, the remaining interest from money invested would provide an income. Father had worked hard to finance his dream, now he and Janett would enjoy the fruits of their labour and wise stewardship.

The land purchased was Forestry land, with two derelict cottages, measuring around an acre adjacent to Walesby Woods. After many letters and phone calls a tender of £500 was submitted and accepted. I took over Brink Hall farm which was left in trust to myself and my two sisters and the transfer would occur on completion of the retirement bungalow. The final design was approved by my father after certain practical ideas had been incorporated. The bungalow was to face due south so that it would receive full benefit of the sun. A large area of glass roof tiles in the rear of the property let light into the central passage. The large double garage at the west end had the doors recessed six foot under the eaves. This meant the doors would last beyond an average life time. Access into the roof space was through a large counter balanced door in the garage ceiling. A sizeable built-in cupboard to the left of the drawing room fireplace had access from the central passage, in which logs or coal could be stored, this saved trailing fuel into the drawing room.

The conveyance for the fuel was a large coal scuttle on pram wheels, carefully made out of 20 gauge tin, riveted and suitably strengthened. This still resides in the garden shed, a monument to a man to whom recycling and forward planning was an art form.

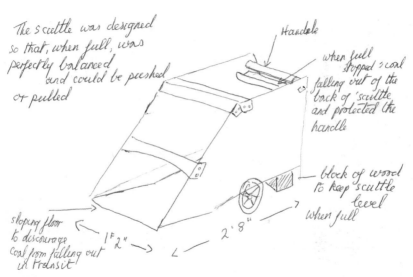

The scuttle was designed so that, when full, was perfectly balanced and could be pushed or pulled. Sloping floor discouraged coal from falling out in transit. Handle, when full, stopped coal falling out of the back of scuttle and protected the handle. Block of wood to keep scuttle level when full.

Larders or store cupboards were common in most houses in the 1960s. Forest House was no exception, with a slight difference. It was common practice to include a larder in the north wall of a house. The larder at Forest House (because the kitchen was on the south wall) was sited in the centre of the building. Cold air reached the larder through an underground tunnel via an air brick in the north wall. Larders or store cupboards were from an age before fridges and were designed to keep certain foods cool.

Forest House

For many years Mother and Father enjoyed their regular walks with three dogs in Walesby Woods. Father had permission from the Forestry to collect fallen wood, and with a large garden and a well-equipped workshop there was plenty to keep him busy, not to mention caravanning

and several years at Walesby Church as Warden. His involvement with the 'Wooden Horse' still triggered curiosity in the local media, and he was able to reminisce on these occasions. Three such occasions come to mind. The Lincolnshire Echo invited Father to Scampton in 1975. The Echo records that Father was the camp carpenter. This is a mistake as the official camp carpenter was known as McIntyre in the book 'The Wooden Horse'. McIntyre refused to help due to the possibility of having his tools (which were on parole) impounded by the guards, should they find out his involvement with the escape. In addition to this his job as camp carpenter would certainly be terminated, so Father got the job of building the horse

In 1974 Father was invited to an historic reunion of 503 Squadron. He was unable to attend, but did manage another reunion of 503 at the Royal Hotel, Norwich in 1985, where again (to make sure they recognised each other) they wore buttonholes of Lincoln Green. The talk was of Handley Page Hyderabads and Fairey Fawns, as the four Special Reserve Squadron flyers relived their exploits from Waddington.

503 Squadron reunion, 1985.

There was a rare speaking engagement at the Limes Hotel, Market Rasen. History does not divulge the contents of the talk, but we do know that during an interview he was asked why he chose to retire in a location surrounded by fir trees, which must have reminded him of those three years behind the wire in Stalag Luft III. I do not recall his answer, but I am sure that from the moment of his capture his chances of surviving the war increased greatly, and in some measure he had cause to be grateful to his captors. We as a family are too. I thank God for my father, a truly kind and good man who has left his children and grandchildren with some amazing memories.

In November of 1958 the annual meeting of the Officer Prisoner of War Dining Club was held at the RAF Club, Piccadilly. Among those present were Ollie Philpot, one of the three who escaped via the wooden horse and made it back to England. Aidan Crawley, a squadron leader 'in the bag' for four years, writes in his book 'Escape from Germany' that fewer than thirty of the ten thousand men in prison camps in Germany ever reached Britain or a neutral country and the proportion among other services were no higher. Father, although in touch with Ollie Philpot, was unable to attend this function. Ollie Philpot wrote his personal story of the escape in his book 'Stolen Journey', published in 1950. He recalls a small box with a false bottom that Father made for the purpose of concealing some of 'Jon Jörgensen's dual identity papers. On page 325 he recalls, "*Now for Wings Maw's box. I took it out of my suitcase, and with an old Reich table knife I prised the false bottom off very gently so as to leave no marks. The nails gave easily, as he said they would. Into it I thrust maps and papers which were not wanted on the next stretch. I was thus mildly search proof.*"

There came a time in Father's retirement when his 'parachute knee' caused him trouble and walking became difficult. Later his leg would suddenly collapse

Royal Air Forces Ex-P.O.W. Association

President: Air Commodore C. H. Clarke

*7·55. Henri Pickard·
artist, killed in the
Great Escape*

Social Secretary

H. E. Batchelder, DFM
7, The Glebe, Lavendon
Olney, Bucks. MK46 4HY
☎ 01234-712736

Dear Michael,   19th March 1999.

I do apologise that it has taken me longer to write to you than I
promised - I have been trying to trace a family representative of
Flt. Lt. Marcus Marsh who was the subject of a second drawing.
So far no luck but through the Jockey Club I have obtained an
address at which Marcus lived in Newmarket (in 1965!); he was the
trainer of the Queen Mother's racehorses at some time.   The
present owners of the house, who are also part of the racing
fraternity, are taking an interest in my search and are
endeavouring to make contact with a member of the Marsh family.

Arrangements for Saturday 27th March are that members of the POW
Association will have their Annual General Meeting commencing at
11-15am; this will be followed by Lunch scheduled to be served at
1-00pm.   After Lunch people generally chat in groups then drift
away by about 4-30pm.

The Royal Air Force Club is located at 128 Piccadilly, that is
the Hyde Park Corner end.   The nearest Underground Stations are
either Green Park, which is on the Victoria line or Hyde Park
Corner on the Piccadilly line.   I think Green Park is the
easier, if you choose to travel this route leave the station
through the exit on the north side of Piccadilly and walk towards
Hyde Park Corner, the Club is about half a mile from the station.
If you prefer you can leave the station by the exit on the south
side of Piccadilly and take a taxi to the Club.

I have enclosed a ticket for Lunch - just in case they ask for it
at Reception.   When you arrive I suggest you ask for me and I
will come and meet you.   Eric Foinette, who I know you have met
in the past will be staying for Lunch so you will at least know
someone!   I look forward to meeting you, very best wishes.

Yours sincerely,

H. E. Batchelder.

*The drawing mentioned in H.E.Batchelders letter refers to the caricature of my
father on page 233. The cartoon (a very good likeness) was drawn on 30/01/43.
The location Stalag Luft 3. The artist - Henry Pickard was one of the P.O.W.'s
shot after the Great Escape. H.E. Batchelder had already, some weeks earlier
written to me with the information concerning the drawing.*
The information I have concerning the drawing is as follows;
*This was given to Tom Watt ex R.C.A.F. POW Stalag Luft 3 in Melbourne, Aus-
tralia by Vic Wood Ex. R.A.A.F. with the admonition to please find the owner. I
hope the individual portrayed receives it.*
*Tom Watts dispatched the cartoon to H.E.Batchelder and the rest is history.
I was delighted to receive this precious drawing.*

Fly leaf of 'Stolen Journey' by Oliver Philpot

and so an electric wheelchair was purchased. This he loved and was able to continue his walks through the woods with Janett and Sam the old Labrador. I remember vividly the phone call from Mother, "Mike can you come quickly, Roger is in the ditch with Joan on top of him!" I rushed over (a four minute drive) to view the following situation, but first a brief explanation. Joan was a dear lady who came over occasionally to help my parents. She had set off with Janett, the dog and Father in his wheelchair. They returned from the walk and drew level with the drive to Forest House. Instead of turning left into the drive, Father turned sharp right and headed for a very deep dyke, spanned by a pipe some eight inches in diameter. The chair up ended, depositing my dear dad in the ditch with the batteries from the chair having just missed him. Joan jumped into the ditch and began to haul father up the side of the dyke. Mother had left the scene to ring me up. When I arrived Joan had, by some miracle, draped Father over the pipe that spanned the dyke. Two things happened simultaneously. A lady arrived with six dogs, and a very distinguished gentleman with snow white hair and a smart suit appeared as if from nowhere (he had no connection with the lady and her six dogs). He took charge of the situation and within minutes had hauled father out of the dyke. I do not recollect how we got him back to the house. The gentleman was on foot so we may well have used the lady's estate car to transport him up the drive.

Father was totally unhurt and the distinguished gentleman had disappeared (could he have been a guardian angel?). When we dried father off and placed him before a cup of tea I am sure I heard him say, "Upside down with nothing on the clock". This is a comment that early flyers would have muttered when their aircraft on landing turned over (upside down) and would therefore have no reading on the altimeter (nothing on the clock). The wheelchair and Joan were none the worst for the experience.

Tessa's memories

First remembrance of family life, age 2, travelling to Lincolnshire from Bournemouth in an old blue Hillman, three children, Mother and Father, very long journey in those days, going to the farm he had found for us. Happy Days, they were both very special people.

Throughout childhood he was simply 'My Hero', when I realized how much he had been through in the war, and before, all the amazing things he had done, and survived.

The days must have been long at Brink, the farm, up at six, lighting the downstairs fires, out to see the men, and farm, always wearing loads of layers of clothes. The old cart-horses, riddling taties outside in winter, the Binder for the corn and sheaves in summer. But always finding time for us, wonderful days at the seaside on the Lincolnshire coast, with old rubber innards from tyres to float in the sea. Sandcastles, quite often aeroplanes he made for us to sit in. Wearing my school felt hat to stretch it, ready for my first day at school.

Later on, helping us in his workshop, being let loose with hammer and nails, making small boats. Then when we were the right age, trusting us to drive the tractors and trailers bringing in the corn, even once driving the combine round the field. Showing us how to sail on holiday, and finally teaching us how to drive the car on a disused aerodrome.

He rarely had time away from the farm, but always visited his sister, Dulcie, in Oxfordshire once a year, and going with Mike to the Smithfield farming show in London. Also joining the family in Norfolk in the caravan, if the farm was not too busy.

Christmas was amazingly organised, lots of presents round the tree, as we opened them we would go to Father, he had a long list of names, ours, and all the relations and friends who had given presents, somehow afterwards we all knew who we had to write and thank what they had kindly given us!

On growing up one realised what a wonderful childhood he had at Cleatham and being able to see the first bi-planes nearby. The love he had for that farm, his parents, and later on, flying, especially meeting my mother, Janett and her family. All the hardships of war, then the happiness of finding his farm. Finally finding a very special retirement bungalow and helping to design it. Always busy there, gardening, collecting wood from the forest, and caravanning with Mother, the dogs, and their friends, the Turners.

His love of cats as well, the farm was always full of cats and special ones followed on at the bungalow, ginger twins, Slim and Jess (after cowboys on tv).

Later on too, the grandchildren from the three families, eight altogether, and the most magnificent tea parties with them all together. They were wonderful grandparents. Also the older boys he would teach to drive along the sandy lanes near Market Rasen.

They left us with many happy memories, and always remember the Air Force sayings, 'Press on regardless', 'chocks away' (the wood against the wheels of the old aeroplanes), 'Piece of cake' meaning you could achieve the task, or already had done! That generation had tremendous spirit and will to get the jobs done. We will always be forever grateful for all they did for us.

Looking back on our father's eventful life, it is obvious to the family, and those who knew him well that he was a modest man, who simply got on with life and tackled each challenge to the very best of his ability. This combined with a great sense of humour, enabled him to meet the difficult sections of life head on.

When asked the secret of his success my father replied.

"It took years of constant practice and self denial.!"
There is no answer to that.

Wapitis, Wellingtons and Binderband

Wapitis, Wellingtons and Binderband